AF570794

Art Media Series

Creating with Colored Paper

Lothar Kampmann

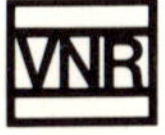
Van Nostrand Reinhold Company/New York

Illustrations

The work reproduced in the first part of this book is by students at the Dortmund branch of the Ruhr Pedagogical College, and by the author. That reproduced in the second part of the book, beginning on page 49, is taken from the collection of the Ruhr College Teacher Training Schools, and the Pelikan Archives. A few examples were also lent by the Karl-Rehbein School for Girls, in Hanau.

Sponsored by the Günther Wagner Pelikan-Werke, Hannover; and Koh-I-Noor, Inc., 100 North Street, Bloomsbury, New Jersey 08804

German edition © 1967 Otto Maier Verlag, Ravensburg, Germany.

Library of Congress Catalog Card Number 68-26804. ISBN 0-442-31320-9

All rights reserved. No part of this work may be reproduced or used in any form or by any means – graphic, electronic, or mechanical, including photocopying, recording, taping, or information storage and retrieval systems – without written permission of the publisher.

Printed and bound in Germany
Published in the United States of America 1968 by Van Nostrand Reinhold Company, 450 West 33rd Street, New York, N.Y. 10001.
A Division of Litton Educational Publishing, Inc.

16 15 14 13 12 11 10 9 8 7 6 5 4 3

Foreword

Today almost every sort of paper is coloured in one way or another, from wrapping-paper to the illustrated press, from notepaper to newspapers. After festivals such as Christmas there is coloured paper all over the house. It is too good to be thrown away. It cries to be used again and should be collected and sorted by colour to form an incredibly rich palette of every shade, for use in creative design.

We shall never lack an abundant variety of shades; it is only when larger areas of any one colour are required that we shall have to set about procuring them. But coloured paper can easily be produced at home using a broad paintbrush or a rag soaked in paint. Any paint will do: opaque paint, tempera or poster paint, even home-made colour mixed from powders and oil. Wax crayons will also serve the purpose.

Do not overlook 'old', unsuccessful or out-of-date paintings which can easily be worked up and used as coloured paper. Ready-made coloured paper can also be bought in a wide assortment: glossy, matt or transparent; both gummed and plain. 'Painting' with coloured paper is a very special kind of technique. The colours, as such, are at hand, and no mixing beyond an optical effect in the pointillist manner is possible. The colours intended to produce a new and different one are placed side by side in the form of tiny scraps.

'Painting' with coloured paper consists of producing a coloured surface by organizing spots of colour. We give these spots a fixed place in the picture by gumming them on, and here is one special advantage of this type of 'painting'. As long as our picture is not yet pasted to the background, we can shift the colours about on the surface and postpone the final decision. This gives us more time and opportunity for correction, which is especially useful in schools. Provided we start teaching them in the right way, the children will soon get used to thinking over the final placement of their colours, and will question the rightness of their intention, and whether they still agree with it. This is not to say anything against the intuitive placement of colour which is, of course, quite feasible in coloured-paper work. But it really belongs

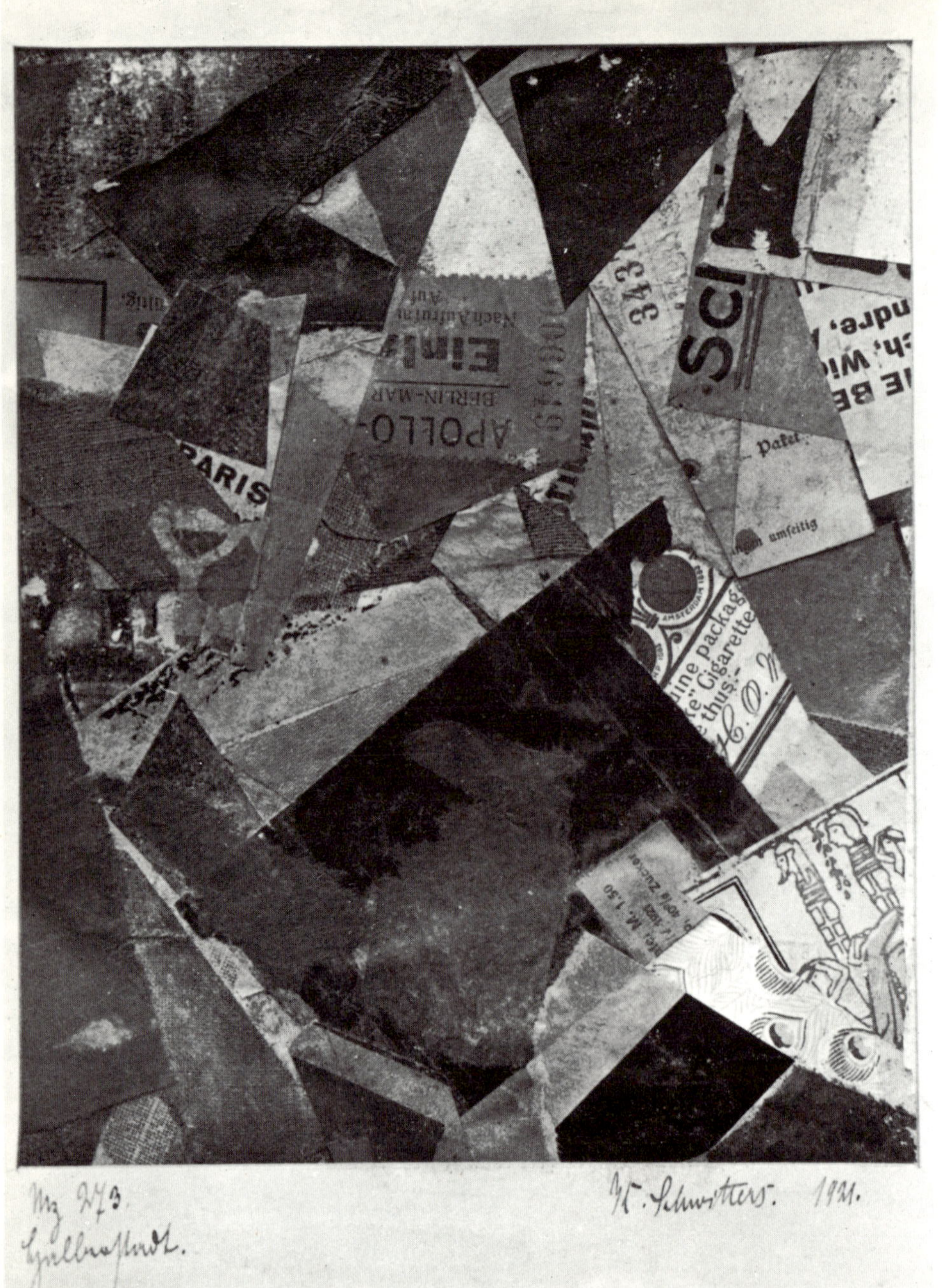
PARIS
APOLLO-
BERLIN-MAR
Paket
umseitig
Gigarette
K. Schwitters. 1921.

to the livelier technique of water-colour painting. Coloured-paper work, with its special technique of arranging and pasting, is an invitation to additive construction, a kind of superposed painting.

Coloured paper is an aid in creative education, and not only by inducing reflection in the placement of colours. It has been so universally adopted that the smallest children can make use of it. But it is more than a plaything, and by no means merely make-shift. It was a long time in gaining acceptance in serious art but it can no longer be ignored. We speak more and more of the art forms of 'collage' and 'décollage'. In addition to its decorative effect, coloured paper deserves a greater educational status in schools, especially in the case of a child who is hampered in his creative activity by his own mental development and the increasing external influences upon him. The use of coloured paper teaches him to design and carry out ideas on a large scale. Even tearing out the paper shapes is not a trivial activity. Conceiving a picture in coloured spots will also bring him nearer to an understanding of painting.

There are four basic ways of obtaining the paper shapes required.

1. The simplest method is cutting them out with a sharp paper-knife or a pair of scissors. Any shape is possible, but they will all have sharply cut edges, which may easily tend to make them look rigid and stiff.

2. Only straight lines can be folded and torn, which limits the possible shapes from the very beginning.

3. Free tearing is familiar to the child from infancy, and things tend to be *torn up* rather than *torn out*, especially when a particular shape is required. Tearing out demands a great deal of concentration, and this is in itself a further educational gain.

4. Any kind of coloured paper can be stamped out with a suitable punch, but the shape to be built up is then definitely limited, if not predetermined, although variety is afforded by the different hole sizes of the punches used. As in all paper techniques, punching allows of both positive and negative work, as well as a combination of the two.

Let us examine the varieties of paper and the diversity of techniques for working with them.

Techniques for working with coloured paper

The youngest children tear up paper with enthusiasm and delight, and strew it all over the room. Those who ignore the essential character of this activity imagine they are witnessing a small human

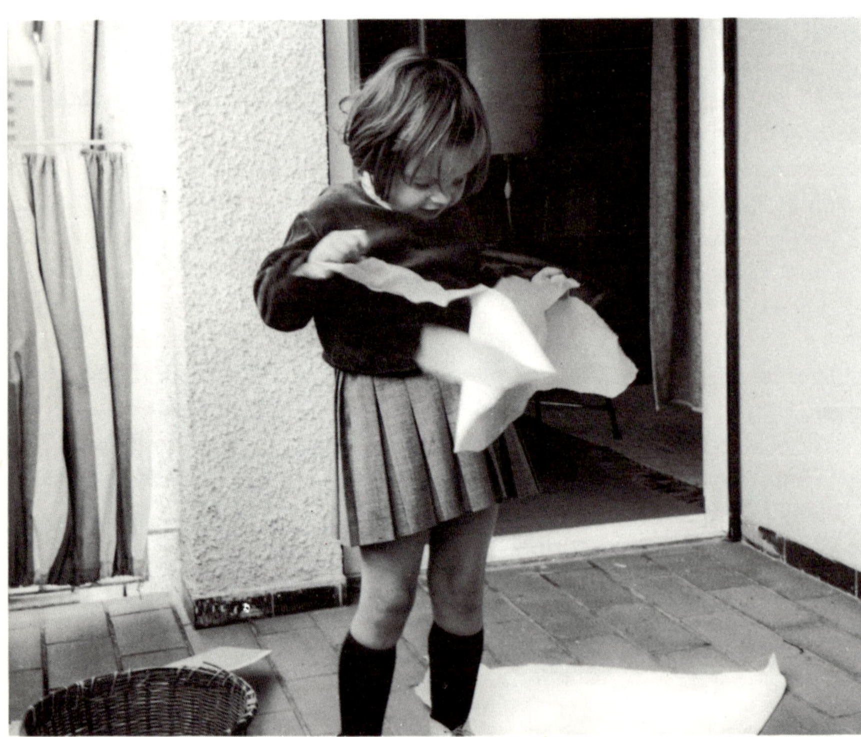

creature's mania for destruction. They do not realize the satisfaction it affords.

Tearing up paper gives the child a particular experience of the world, and of his own capacity for altering it. But, as we said previously, tearing up is not the same as tearing out, which is one of the prerequisites of creative design with scraps of paper. Two others are the capacity to organize and the capacity to discriminate; and a little serious consideration must convince you that these are most important, both for creative work and for life itself.

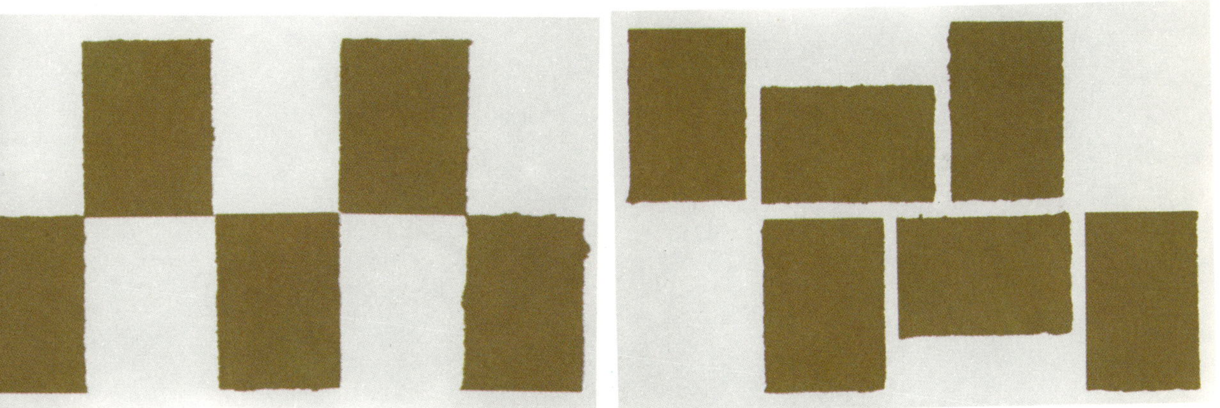

First, organization: arrangement on a surface. Ordinary wrapping-paper will do for this. Learning to put things in a considered order rather than placing them at random and pasting them down in a hurry.

To a small child it is quite an experience, as well as an attractive task,

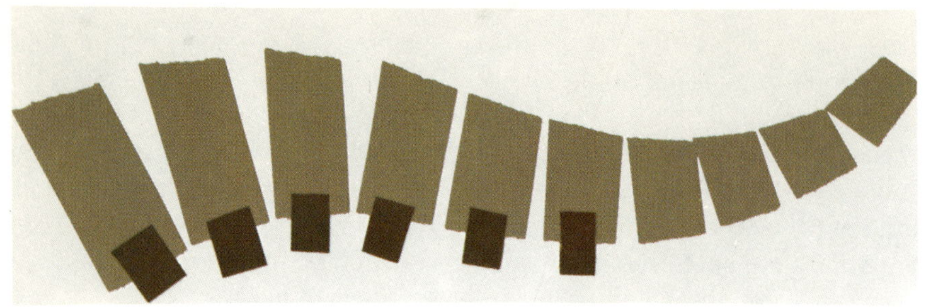

grading things from large to small, from long to short, either next to one another, or overlapping.

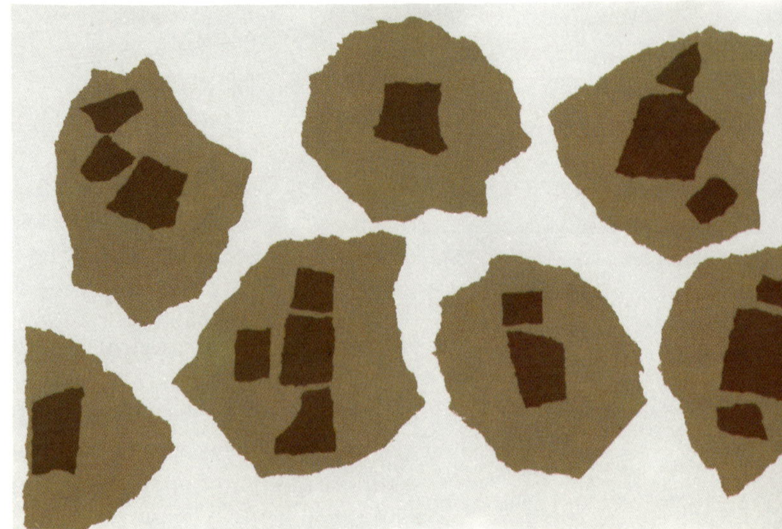

The next step should be co-ordinating large patches, on which smaller ones are to be arranged.

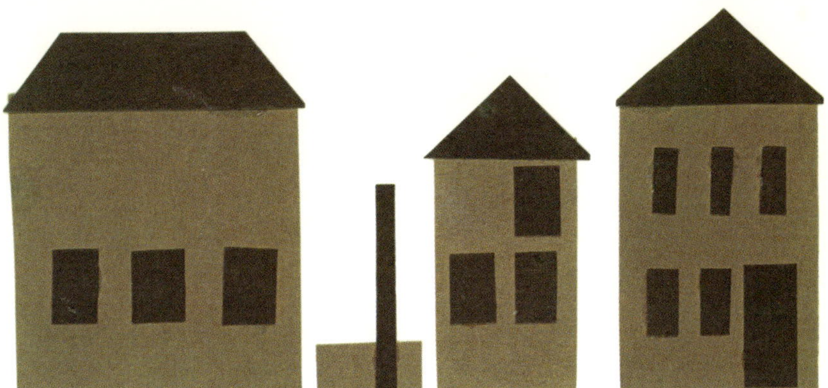

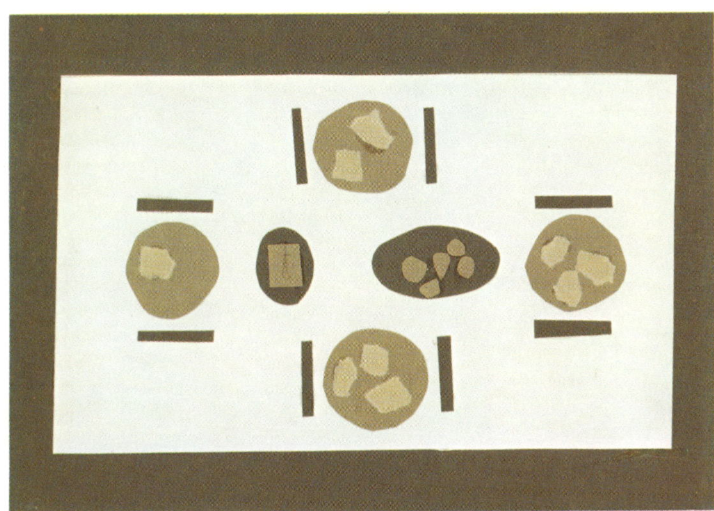

Like the arrangement of windows and doors in houses,

or potatoes on plates, and plates, in turn, on the dinner-table,

or the wheels and doors of the railway engine and its coaches.

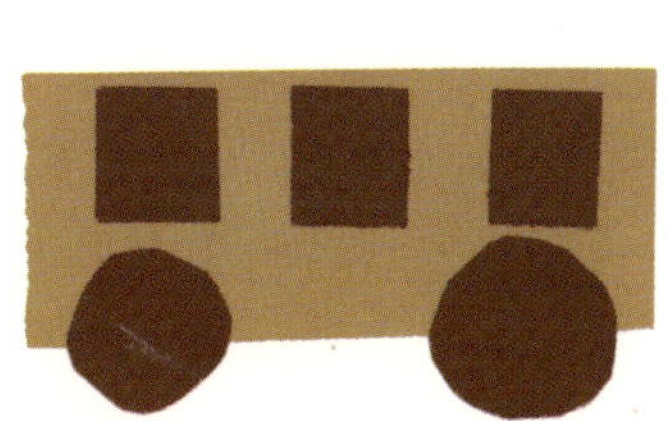

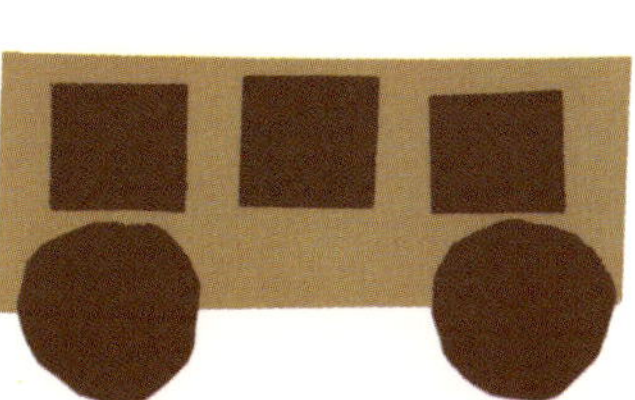

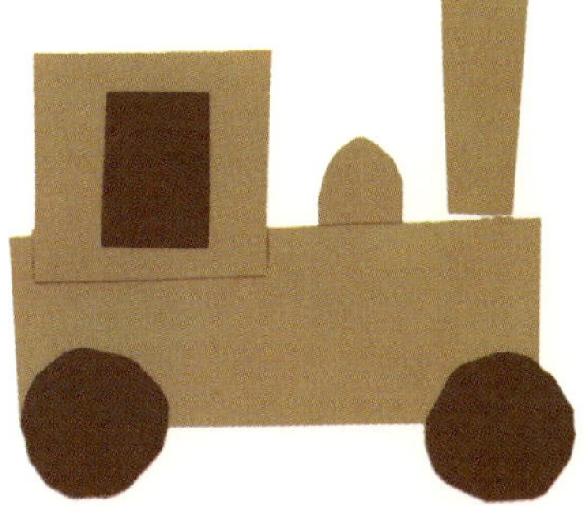

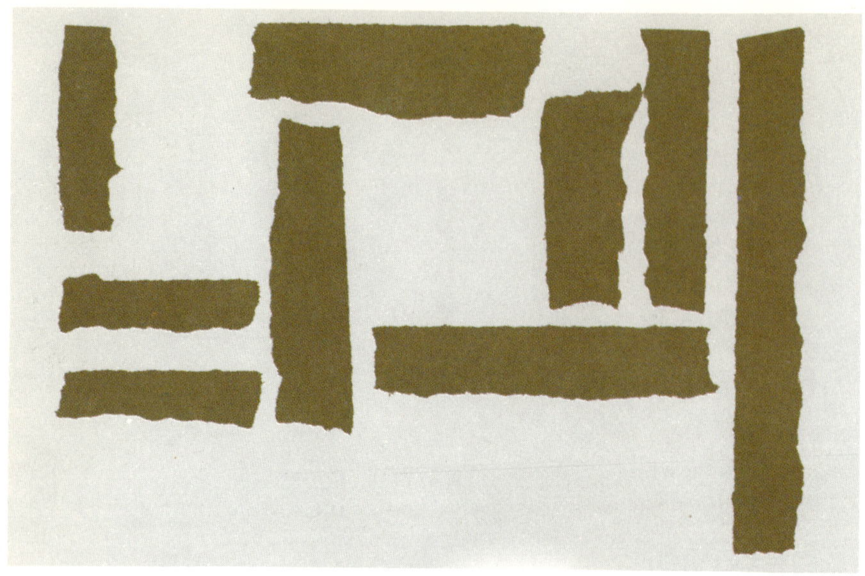

Children learn to arrange things vertically and horizontally,

centrally,

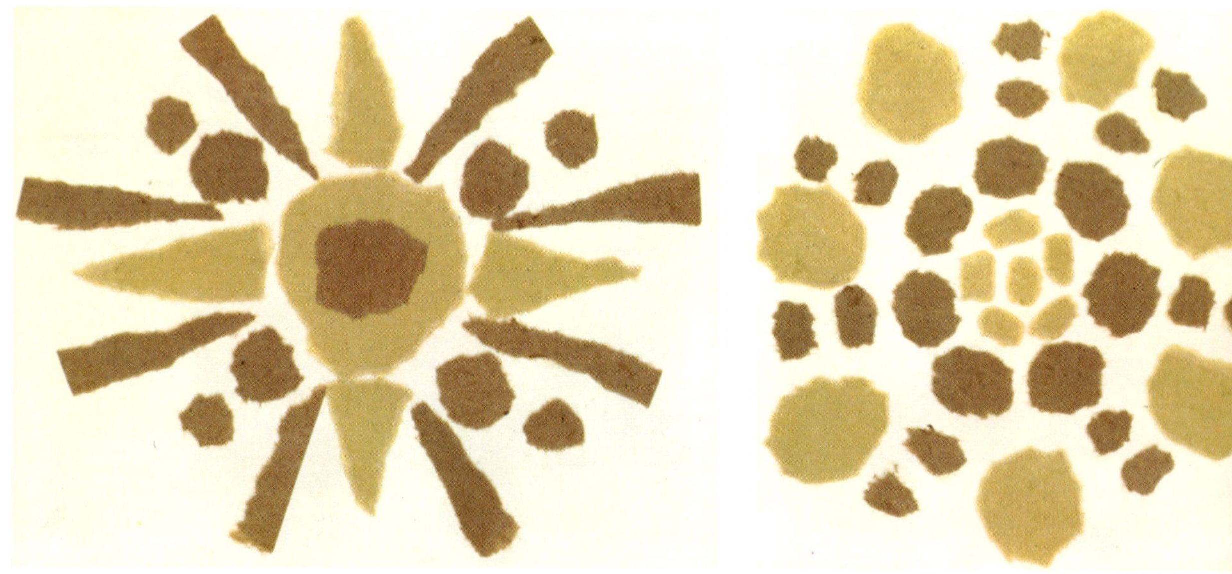

in clusters,

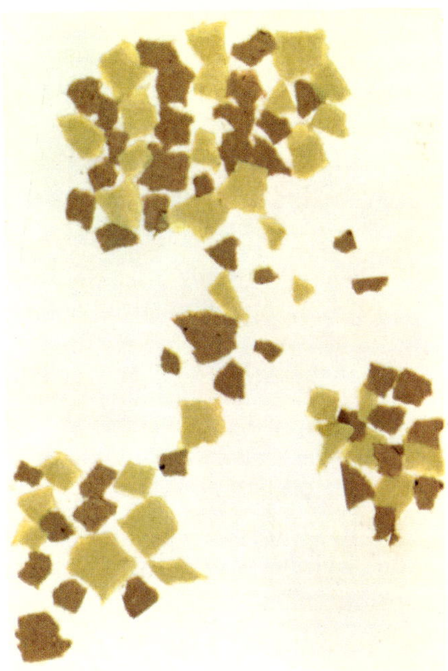

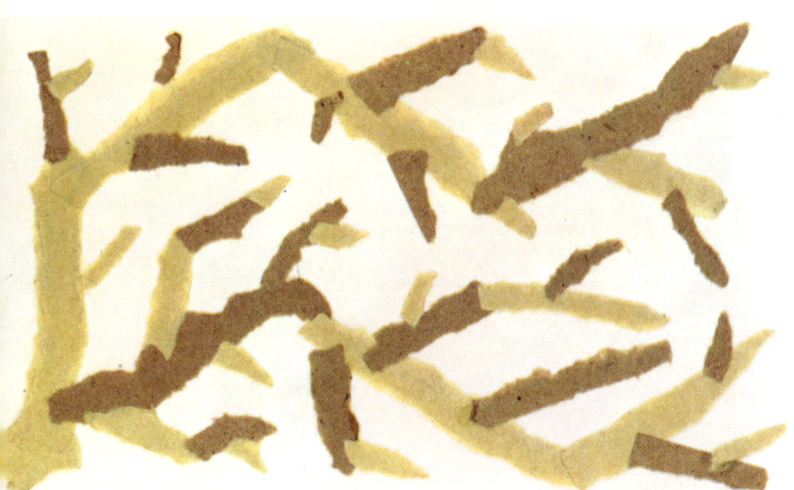

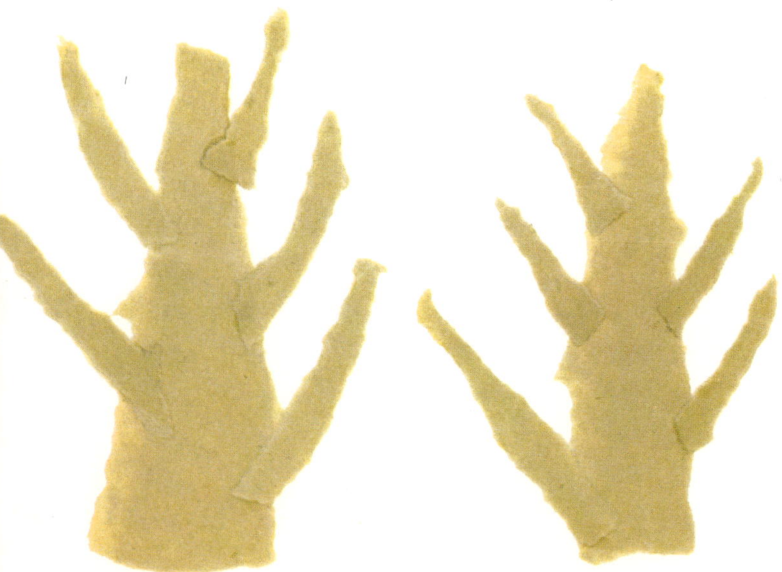

and by branching out. Suitable subjects for all of these should be given. First, differentiation according to size and form, then differentiation according to colour. Prepared for the first task by telling the children to bring coloured paper to school for the next lesson: either coloured envelopes, newspapers, wrapping-paper or their own old, coloured drawings.

The task itself should be assigned in this way: 'We will sort all the papers according to whether they are mostly red, yellow, green, blue, brown or black. Then we'll sort them into light and dark.' A seemingly simple exercise of this kind is fully justified both educationally, and as practice in design. It leads the child to use his eyes consciously and with discrimination, an excellent preparation for any kind of painting. The names to be given to the different shades should also be discussed, although here the chances of agreement become less.

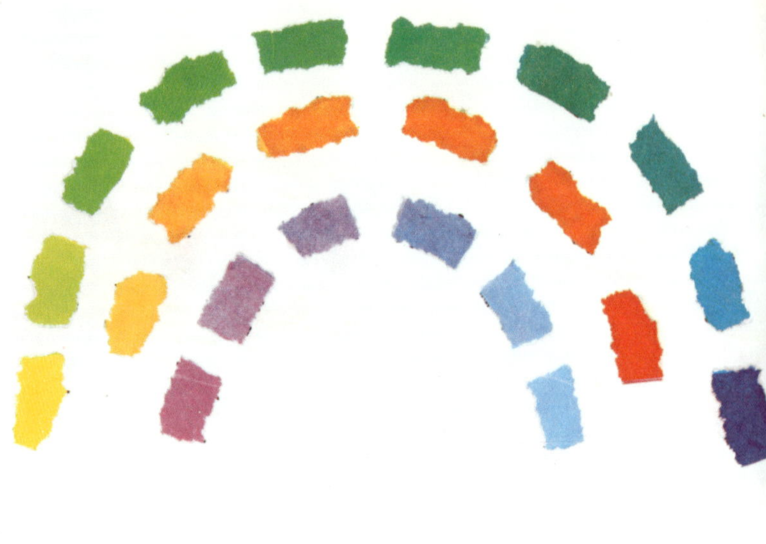

An important function of art education is to sensitize the eye. Dark colours should be sorted out after light ones, red after yellow, green after blue; in stripes, spots and circles.

Attention should also be paid to the practical side of the technique. It will help the child to find his way in working if the different-coloured scraps are kept in separate containers to act as an orderly palette such as that provided by a paintbox.

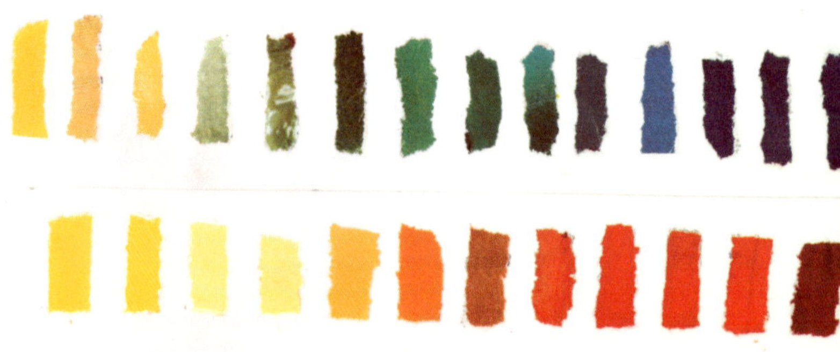

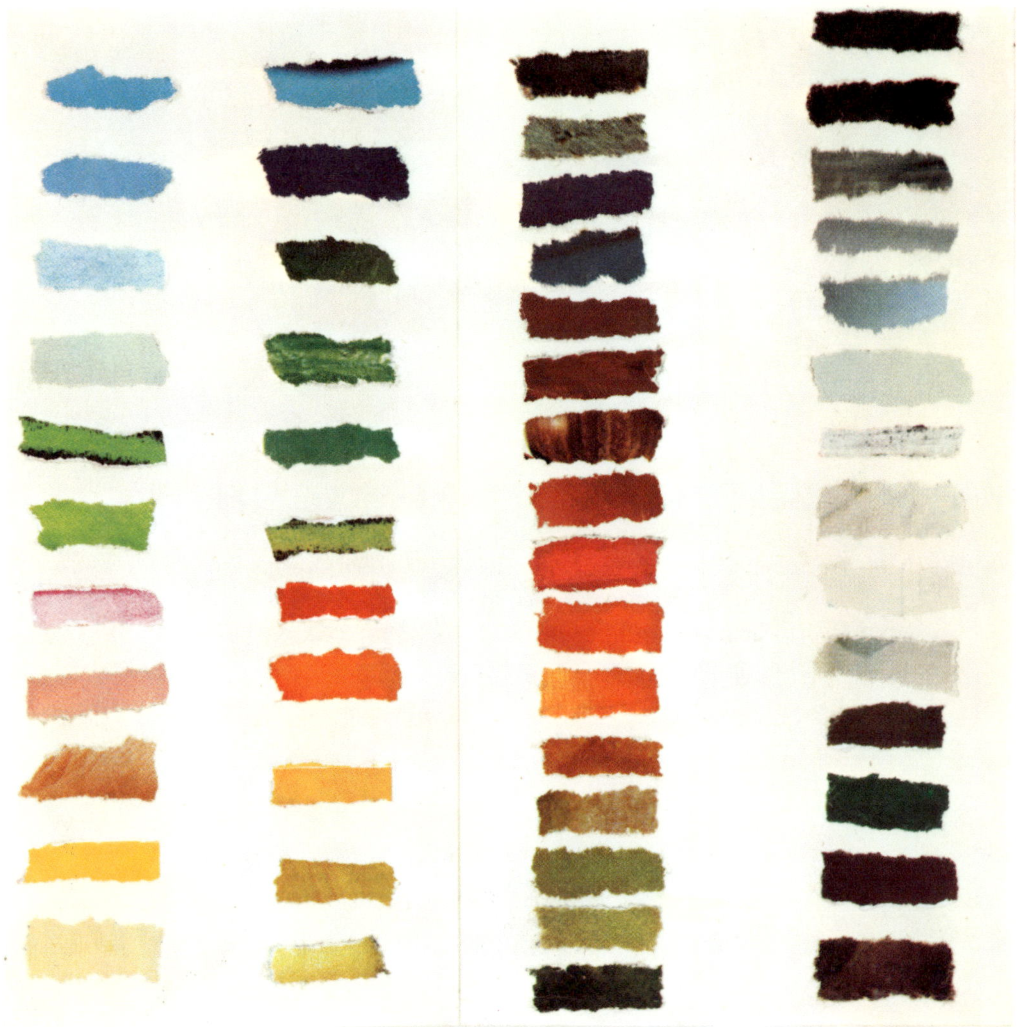

We can borrow the colour schemes of nature: spring, summer, autumn and winter, without having to think at all of a naturalistic representation.

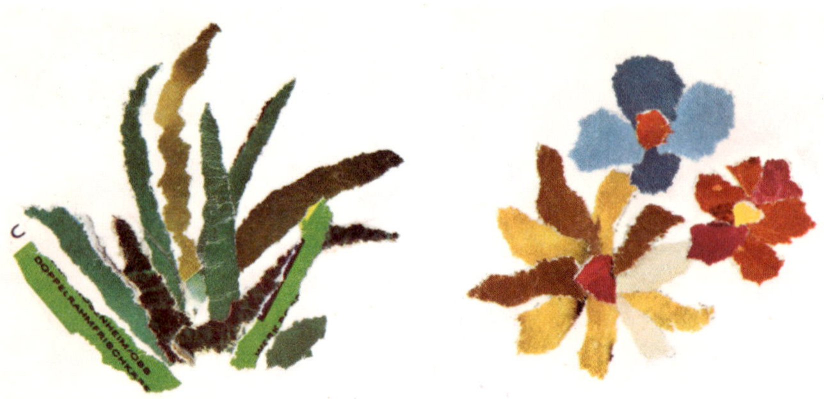

The progression to this exercise will be easier and more discerning after such an exercise in differentiation: the play of green in grass and leaves in the spring, the wide variety of reds and yellows in summer flowers, the wealth of rust and brown shades in the autumn, and the alternation of greys in the frosty landscapes of winter.

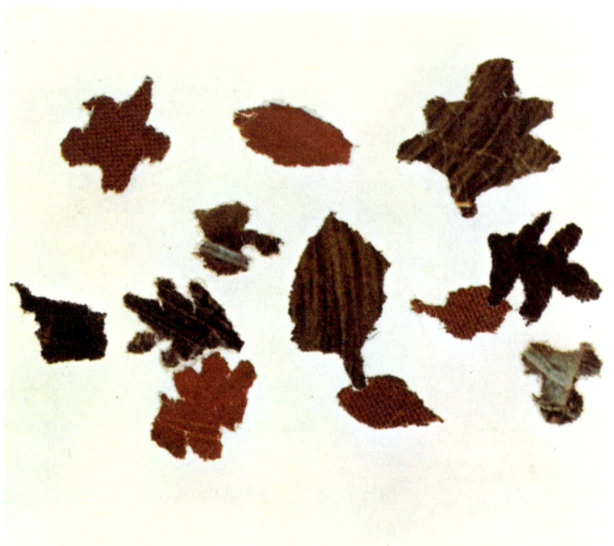

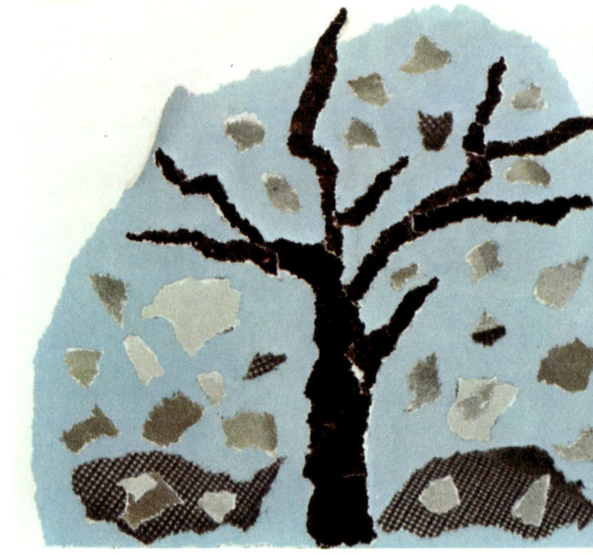

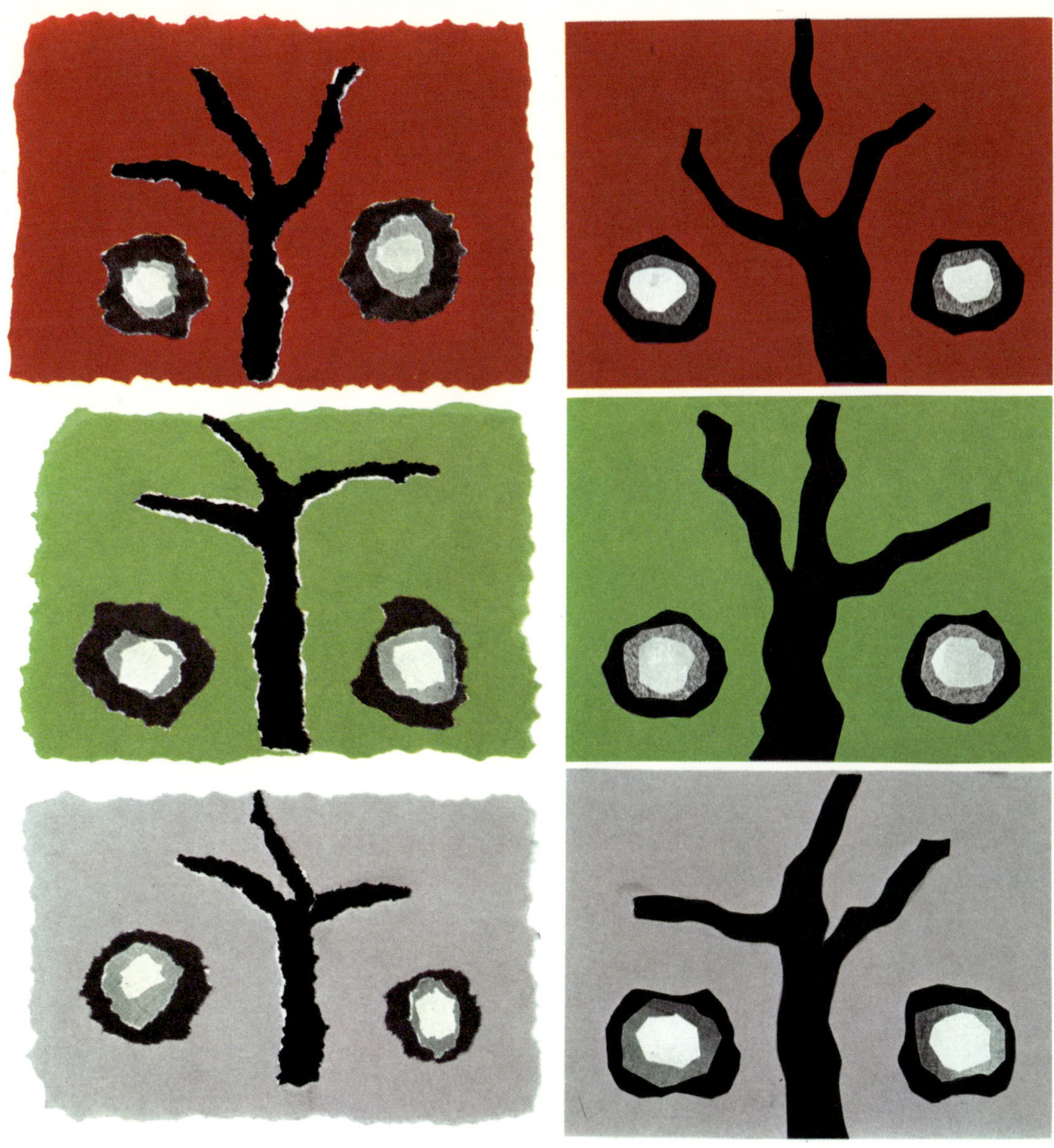

As in every form of painting, the choice of background is important. Each one will produce a different effect on the same composition.

The effect will be different, too, if the design is cut out instead of being torn out.

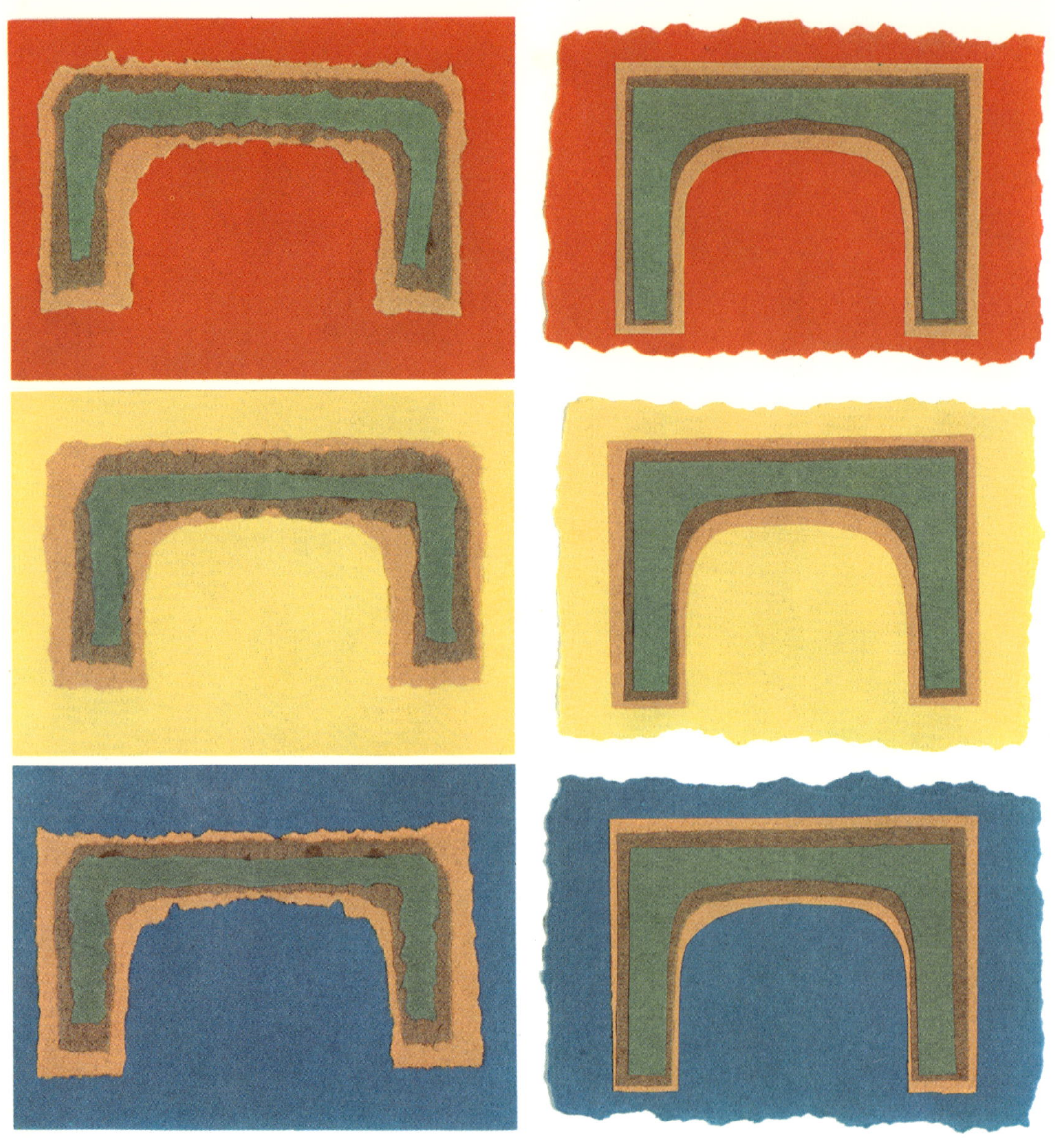

In any case, the deliberate alternation between torn and cut coloured paper is one of the many ways in which the texture of the picture can be made lively and attractive.

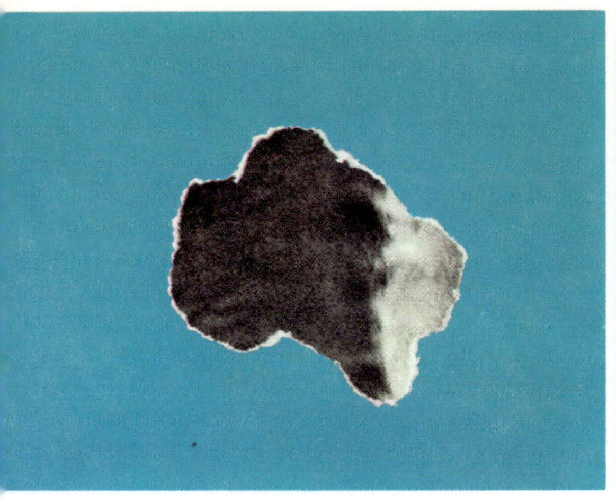

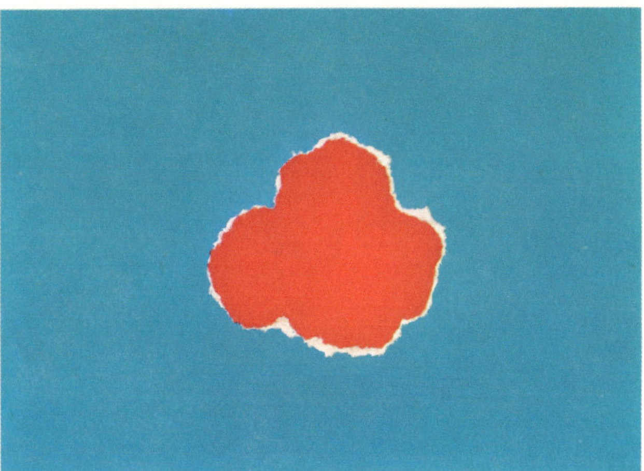

Up to now we have been concerned with torn or cut paper to be arranged and pasted down. But negatively torn or cut paper work can be just as pictorial. The simplest form of this is a large torn-out hole disclosing an underlying sheet. The superimposed negative can produce different effects – supporting, harmonizing, estranging.

Now lay a sheet of transparent paper between the negative *'passe-partout'* and the picture underneath. The colours that first 'quarrelled' are now blended in a common colour scheme.

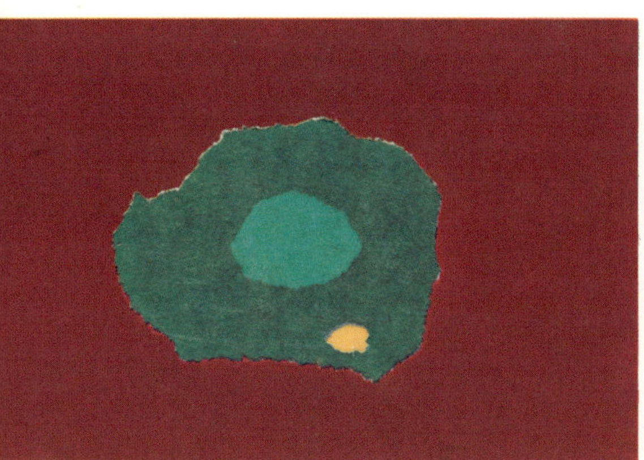

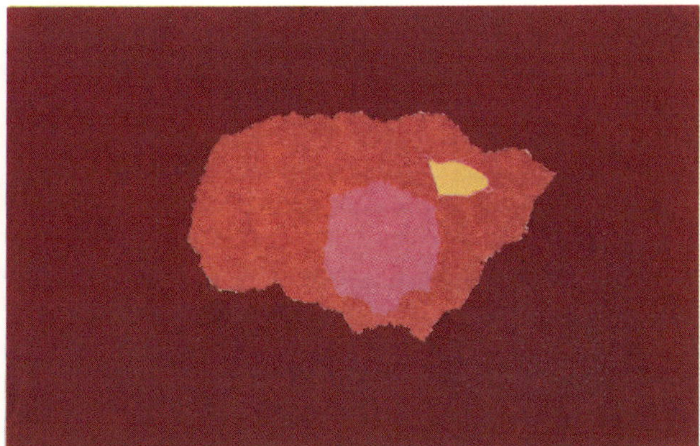

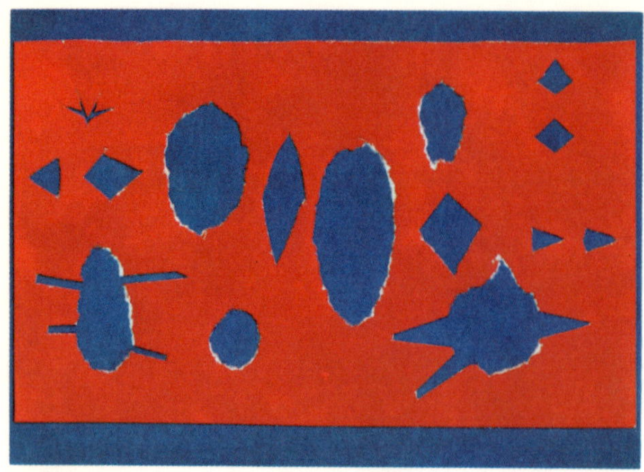

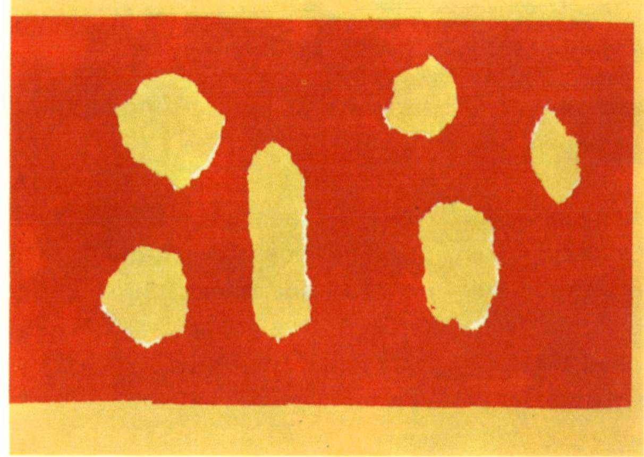

If we exchange the single 'peephole' for a multiple one, we can first compose the arrangement of the 'peepholes', and then, by shifting the position over the same background, produce fresh compositions.

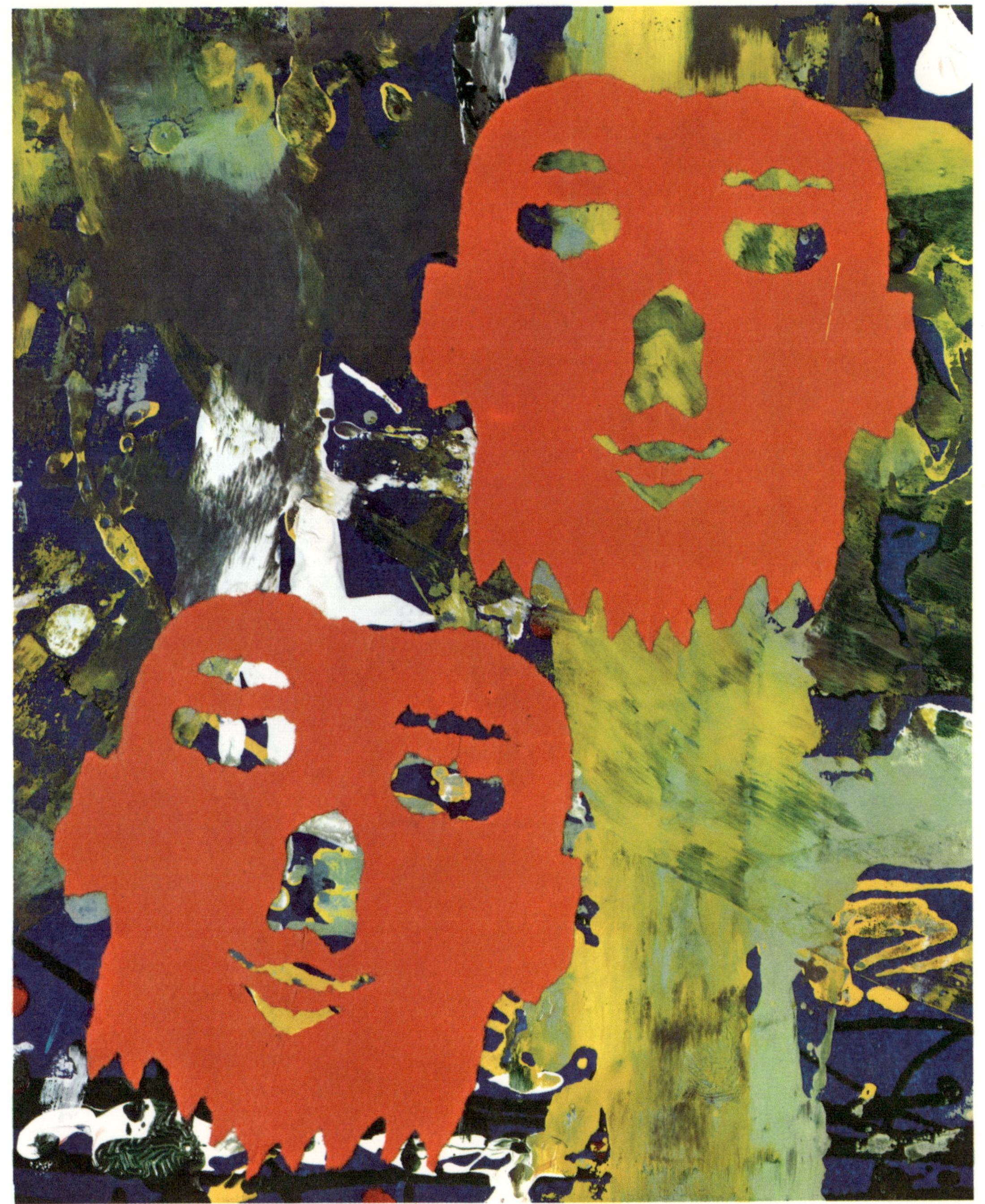

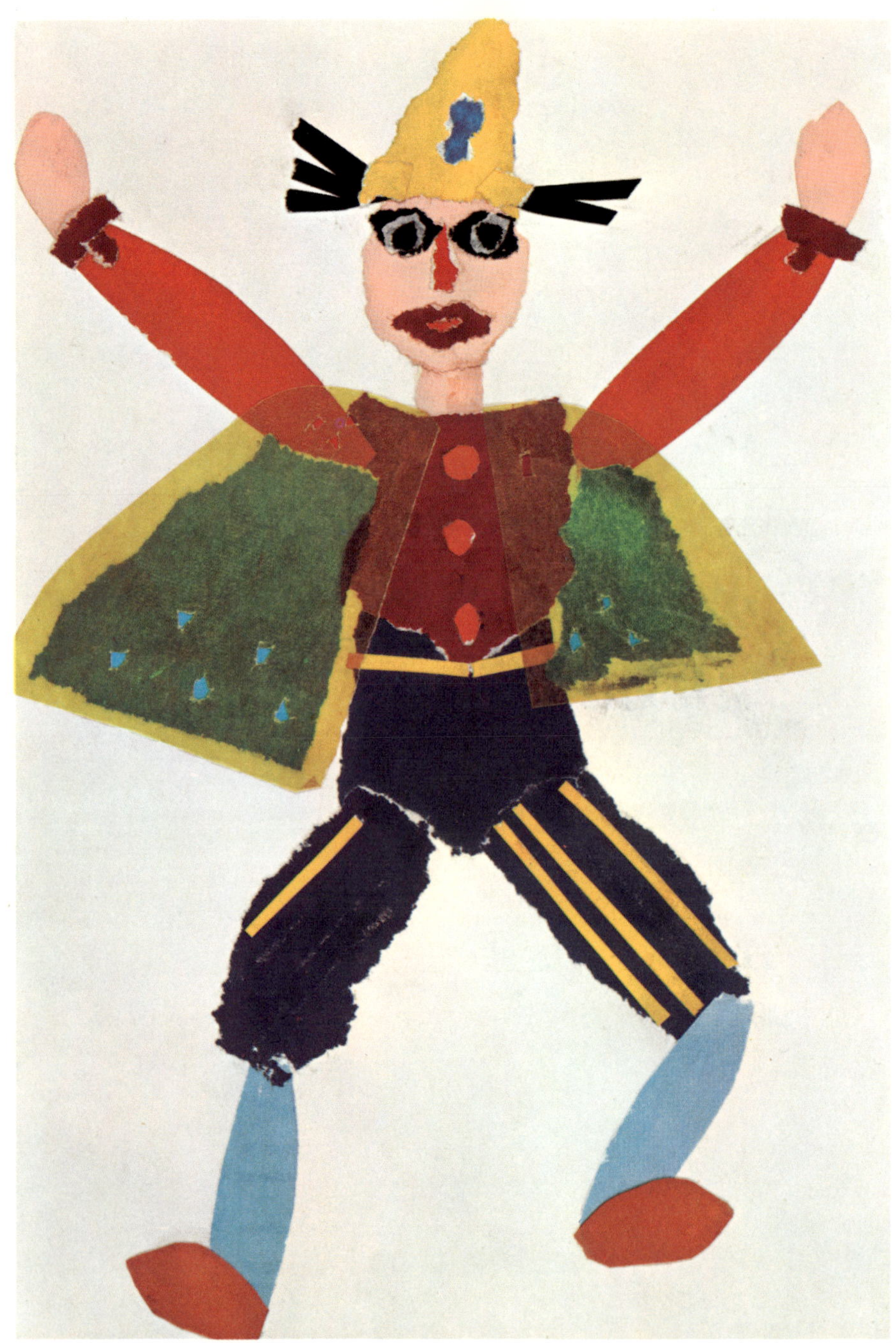

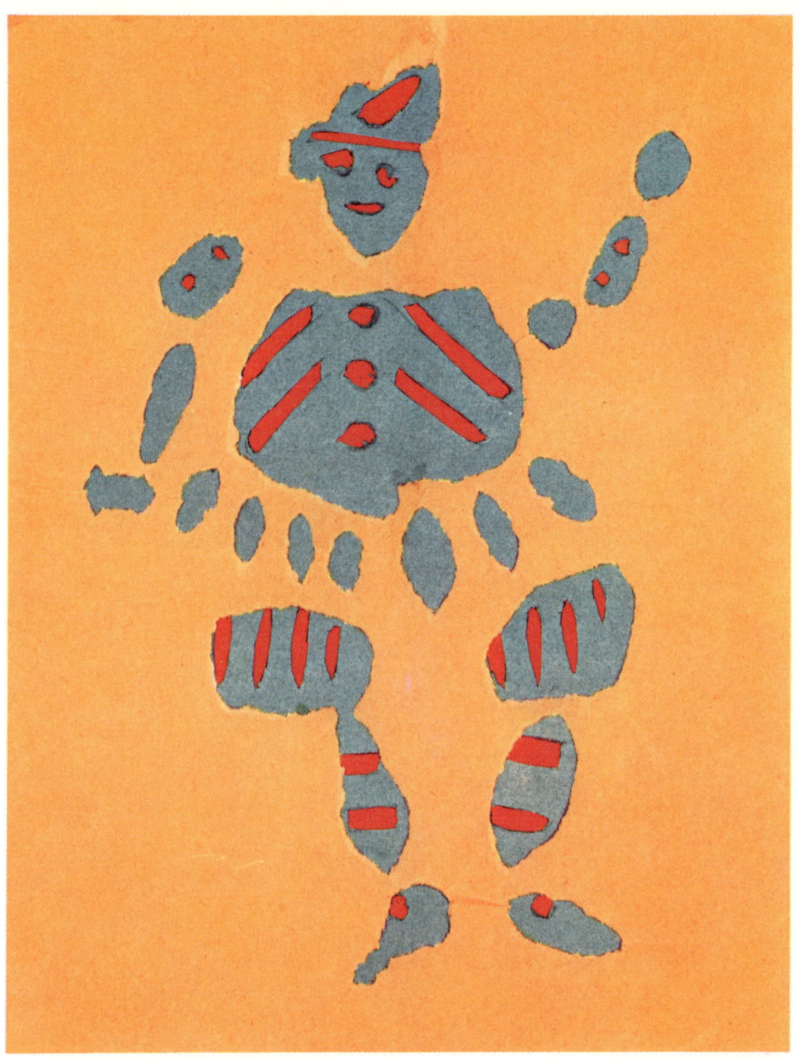

By way of résumé: In coloured-paper work there are two basic methods of organizing colour and form.

1. The successive application of coloured patches, known in the art world as 'collage'.

2. The removal of patches from a coloured ground, to allow the underlying colours to be seen. This process resembles that known as 'décollage'.

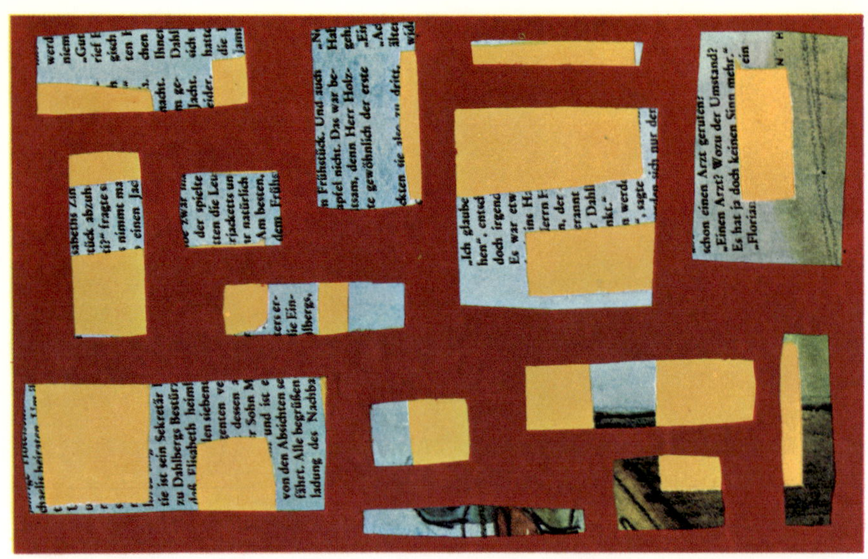

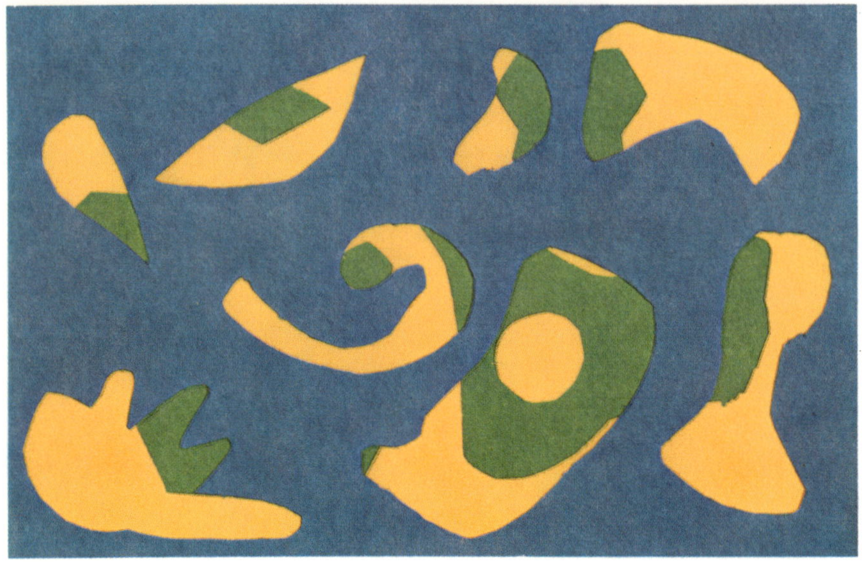

The next step will be to place several negative, torn-out or cut sheets, one over another.

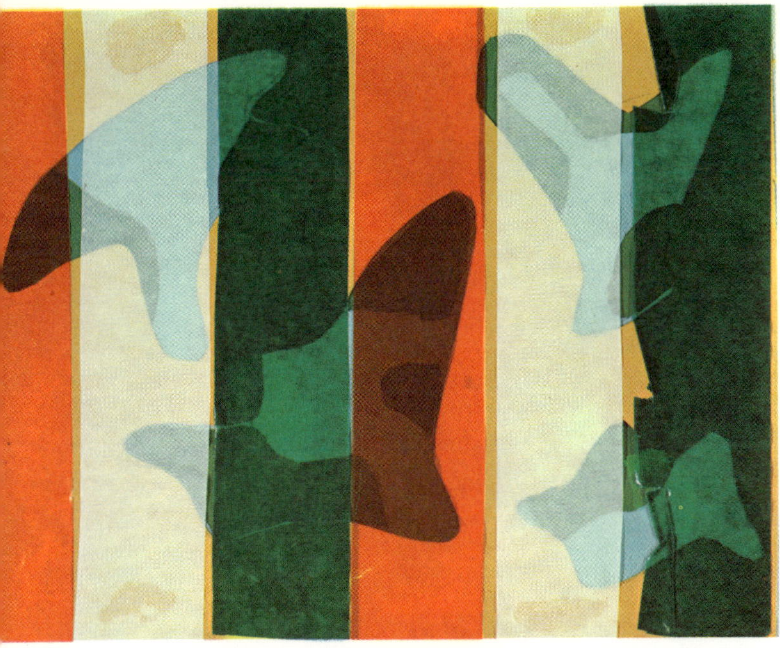

With these two basic methods, sticking patches on, or removing them, all sorts of creative schemes can be carried out. We use the same technical principles—tearing or cutting—while shifting the pieces until the right combination has been found, and then glueing them down.

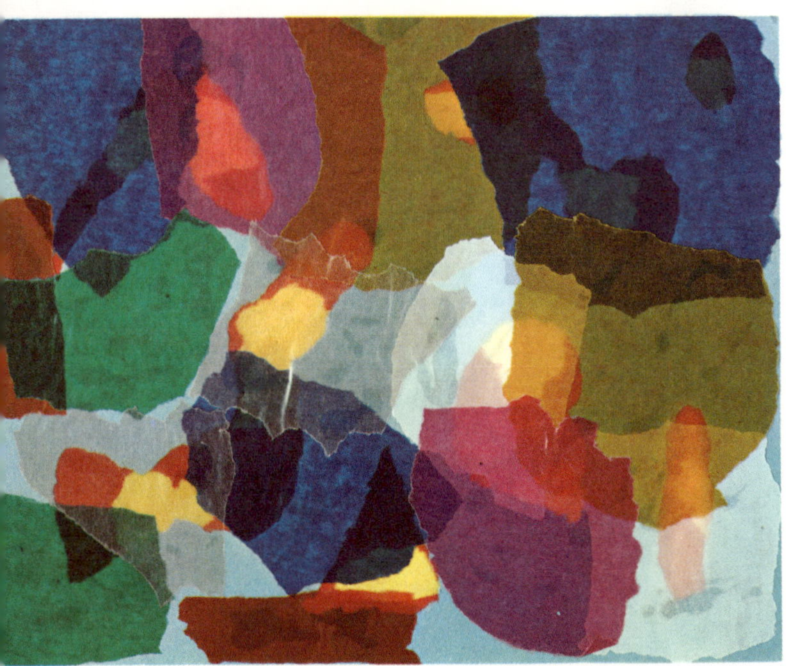

Up to now we have considered only opaque paper, but all the foregoing applies to transparent paper as well. The optical effect, however, will be as different as that between opaque paint and thin watercolour, or paintings on canvas and stained-glass windows.

Transparent coloured paper can be seen through, and this must determine the way in which it is used, both technically and creatively. We have seen the way in which a design can be 'pulled together' into a uniform colour scheme by placing transparent paper over it. It is just as possible to co-ordinate different patches of transparent colour over an existing design.

Some elementary exercises will enable us to make a sampler of colour variations. The strength of a colour is intensified by folding the paper. But when working with transparent paper over a white ground, only light-coloured paper, letting a great deal of light through, will be effective. Folding can give a structural appearance to a surface,

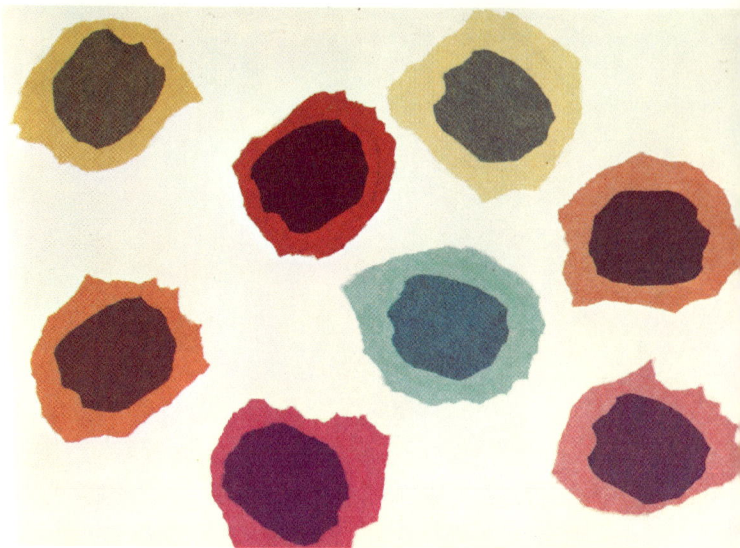

or produce a pleated figure.

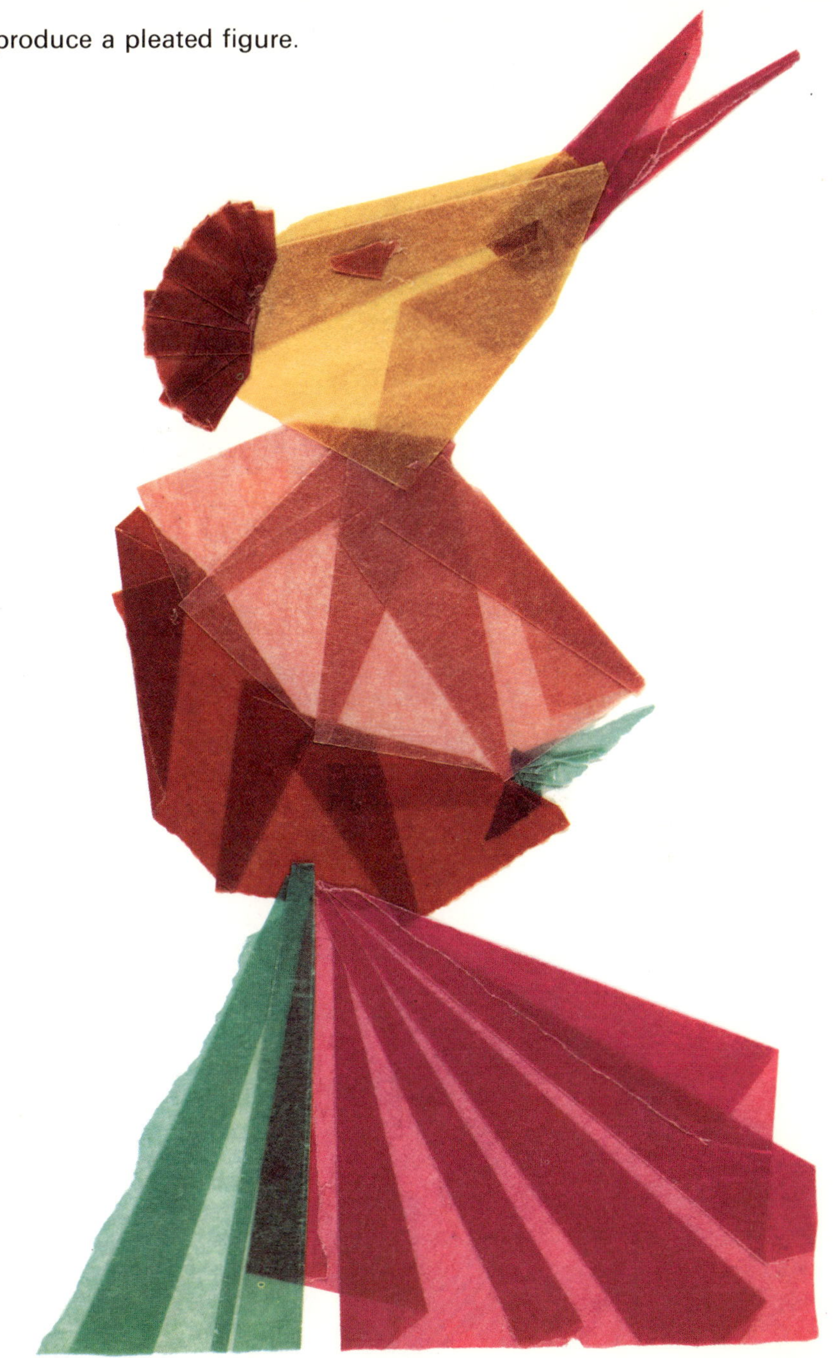

But if the colour value of the transparent paper is to be put to the utmost use, the design itself must be transparent throughout. We must treat it as we should coloured glass. This can be done in different ways.

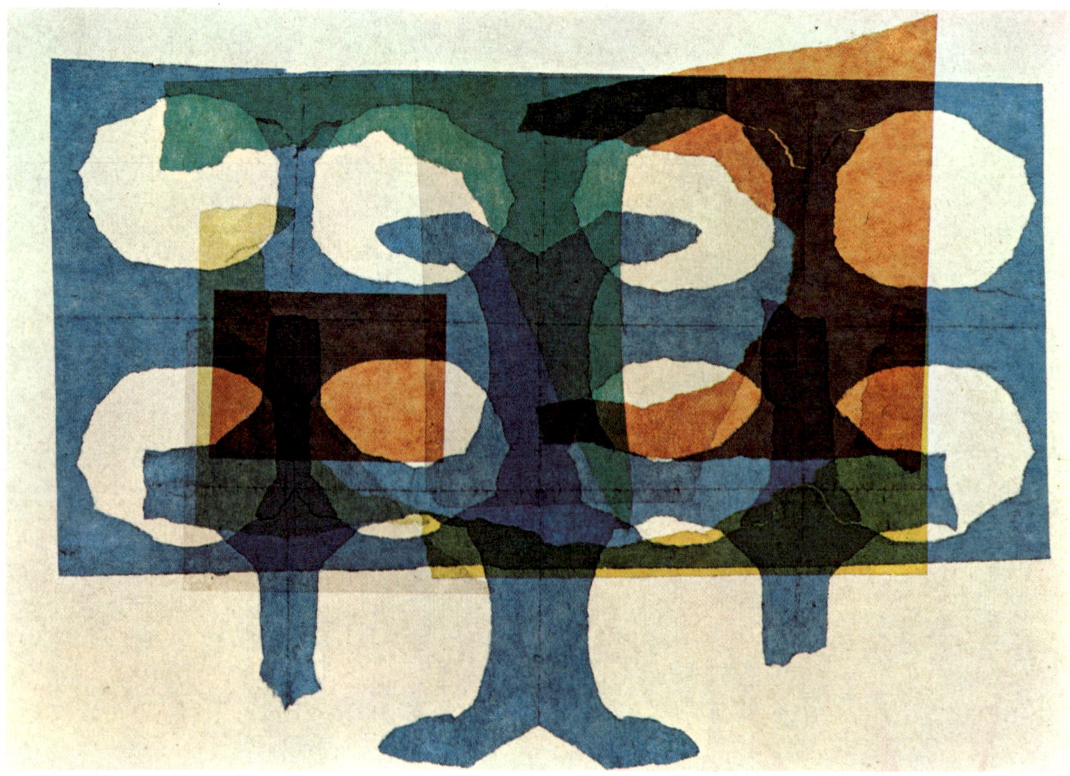

We may take colourless tracing paper such as architects use, as a base (ordinary waxed paper will do), and work over it with transparent coloured paper.

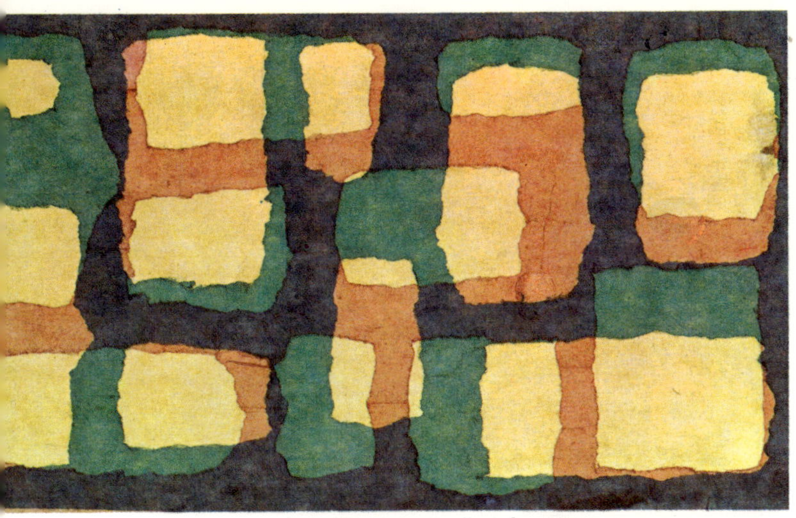

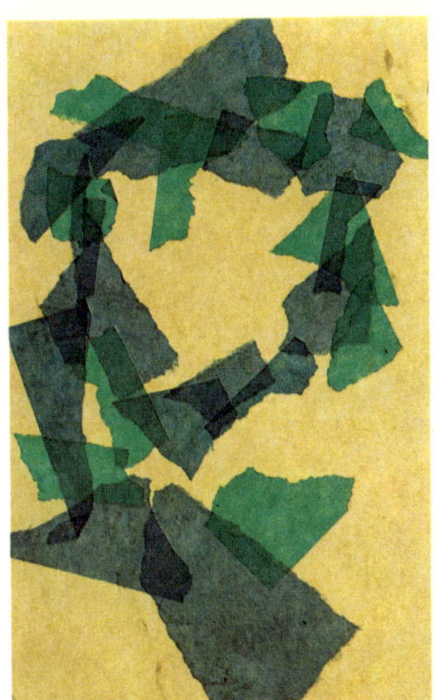

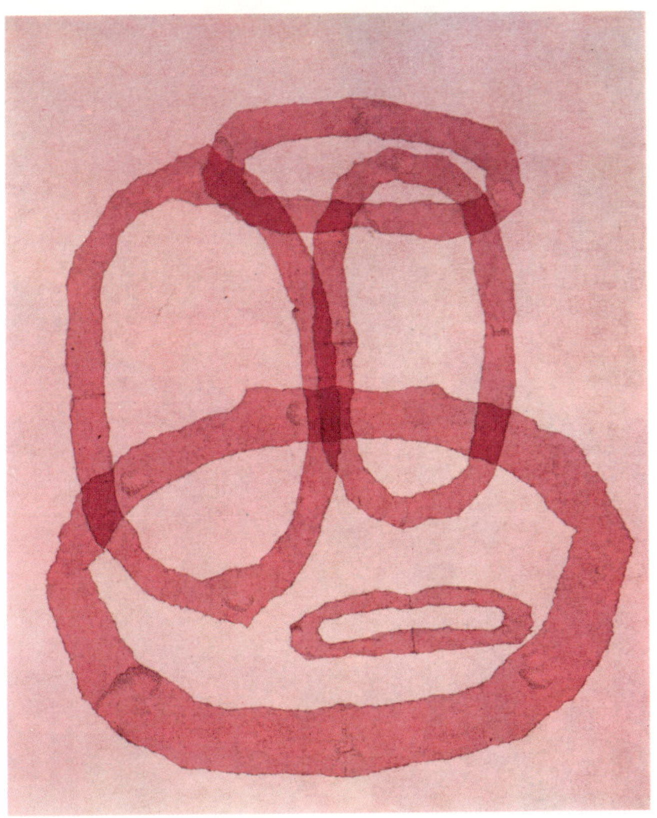

We can also use coloured scraps on a coloured ground.

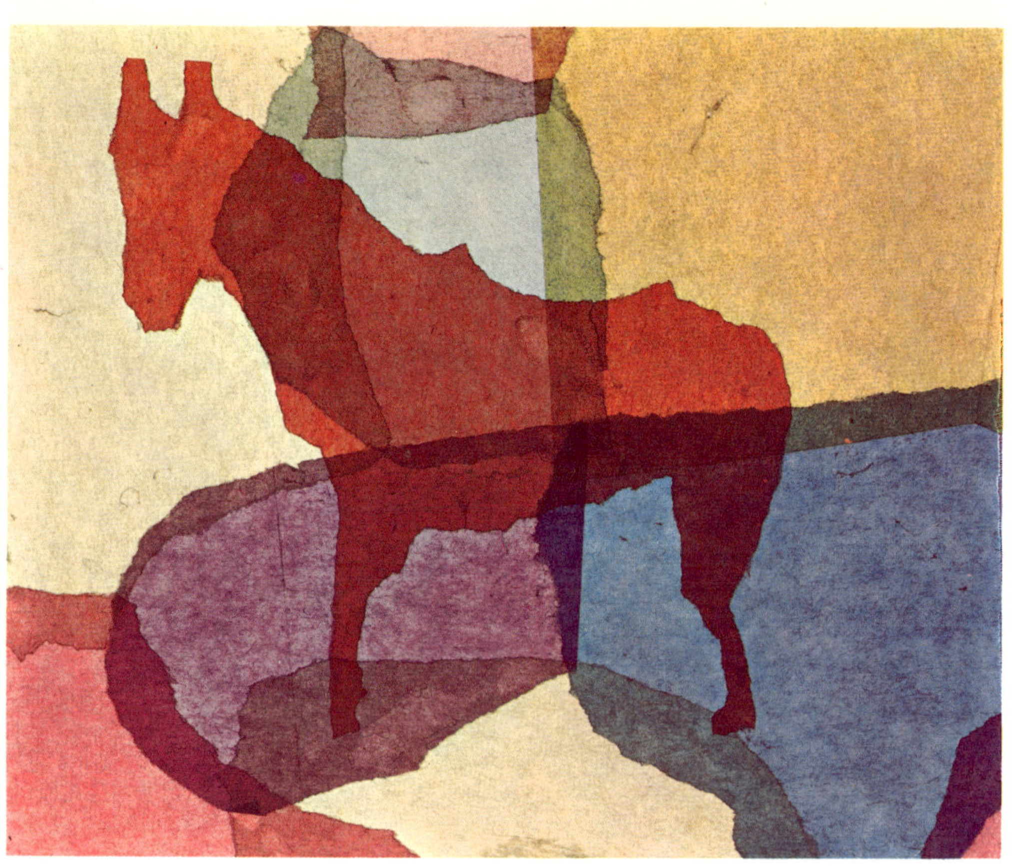

Next, we can make the background of several different pieces, and then place other coloured patches over it.

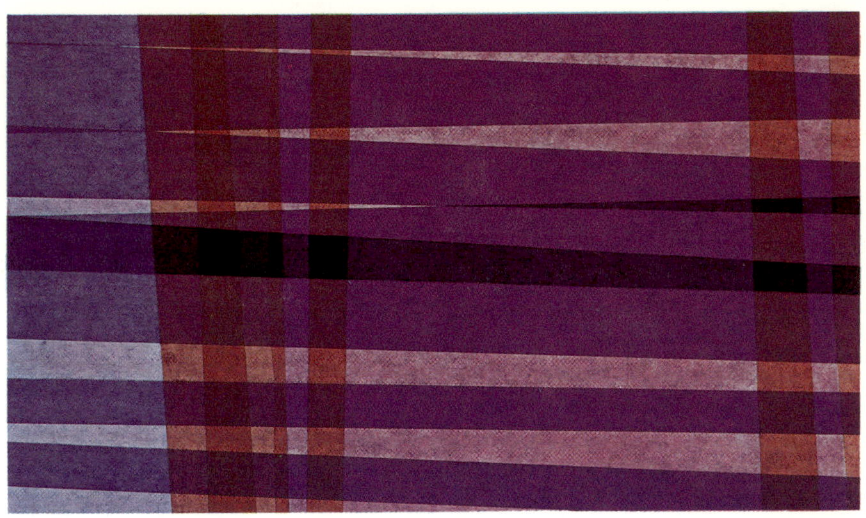

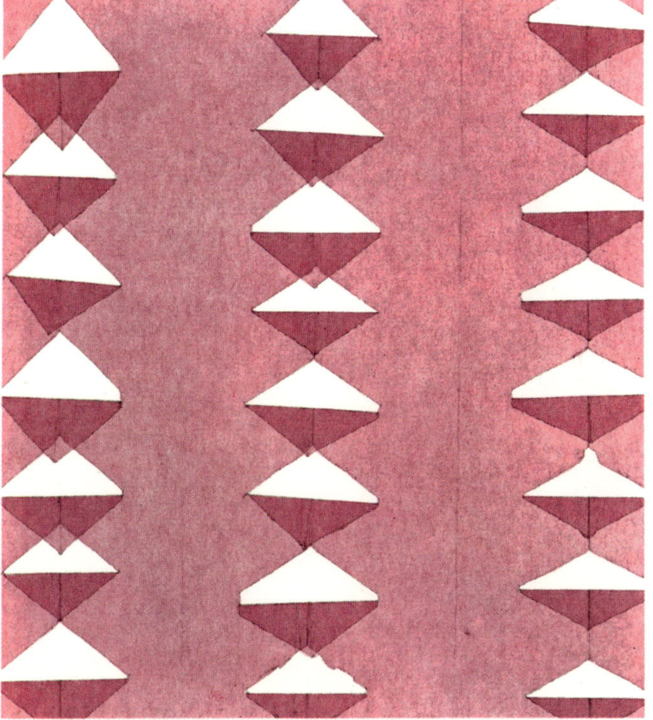

Now we get the full effect of folding the transparent paper. The resulting pictures are best seen against the window in daylight.

While we are on the subject of folded transparent paper, notice the decorative effect of allowing the light to play its part, by cutting through the paper and folding it back.

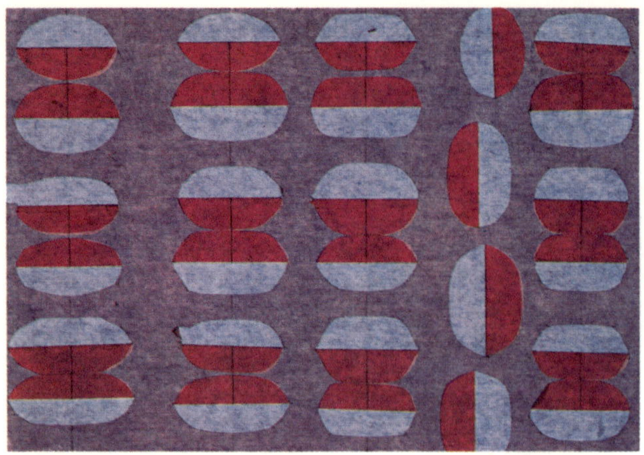

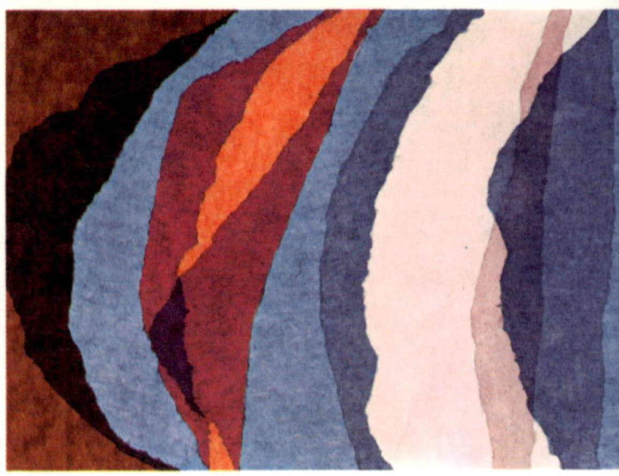

The same technique will have a new effect if carried out in one colour on a different-coloured transparent background.

Overlapping colours can be organized within an enclosed area,

or used to form designs within an organized area.

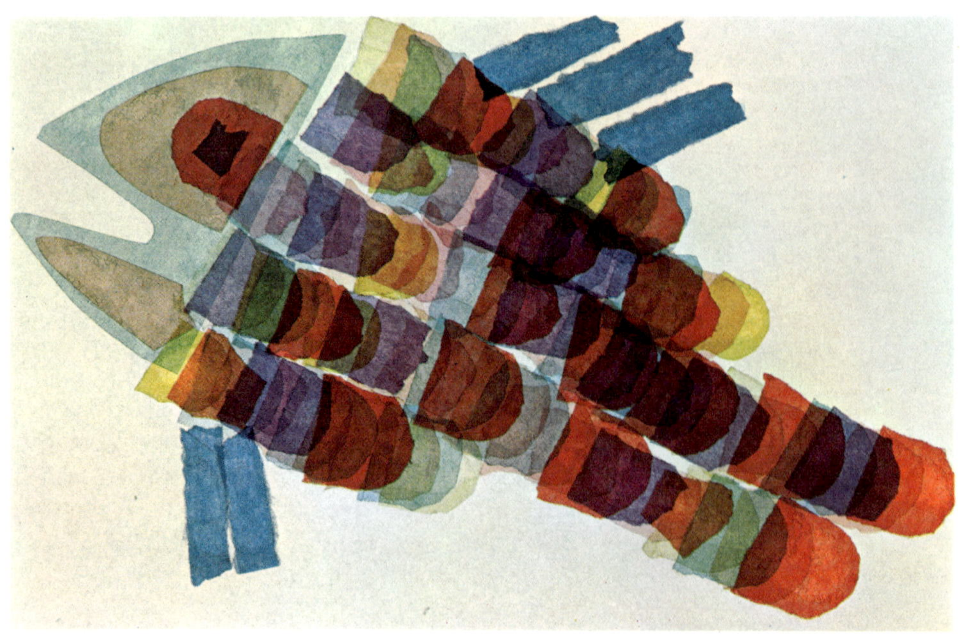

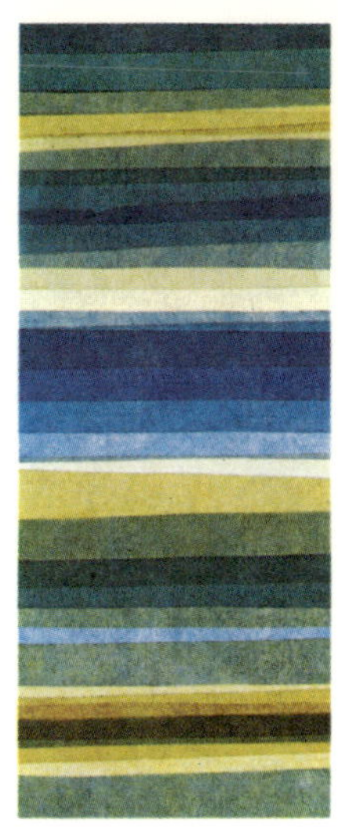

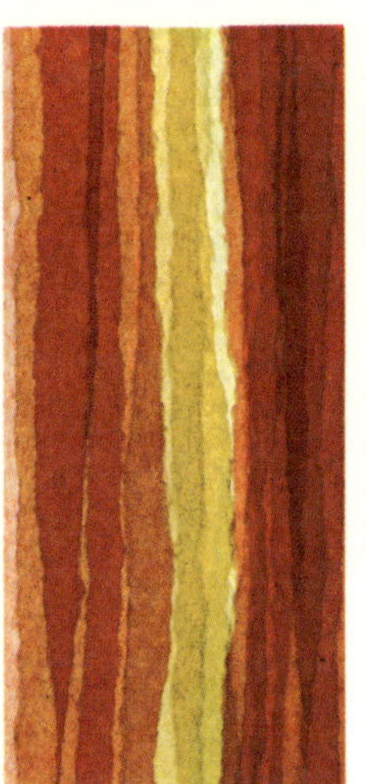

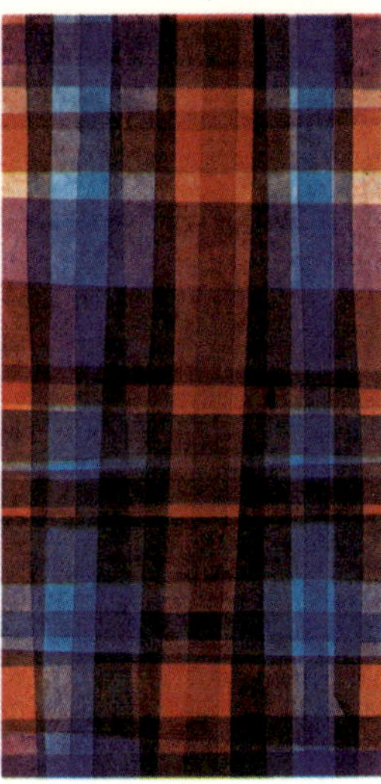

Designing with transparent paper is one half of this exercise, and combining it with a talk on the laws of colour is the other, equally important half. This is the best opportunity for a convincing demonstration of the fact that blue and yellow make green, red and yellow make orange, and red and blue make violet.

The subtle connection between colours which comes to light in the course of their work, encourages the children to talk about new shades they have discovered.

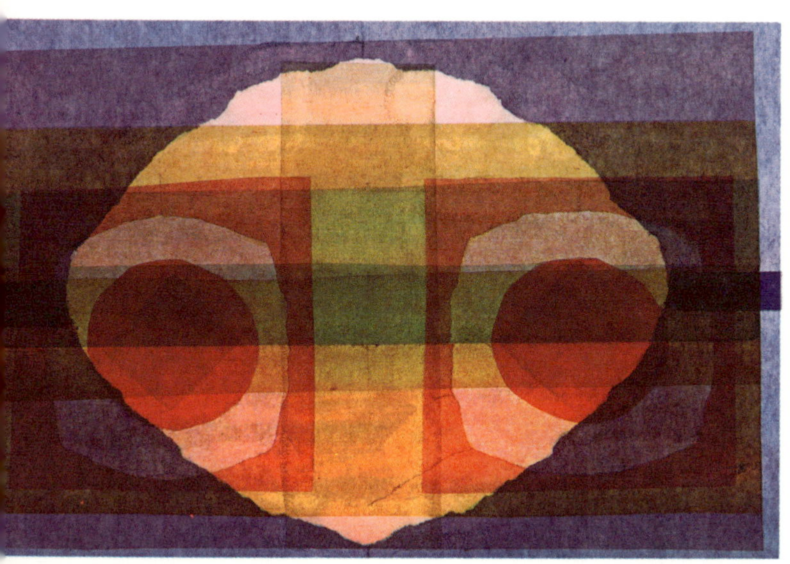

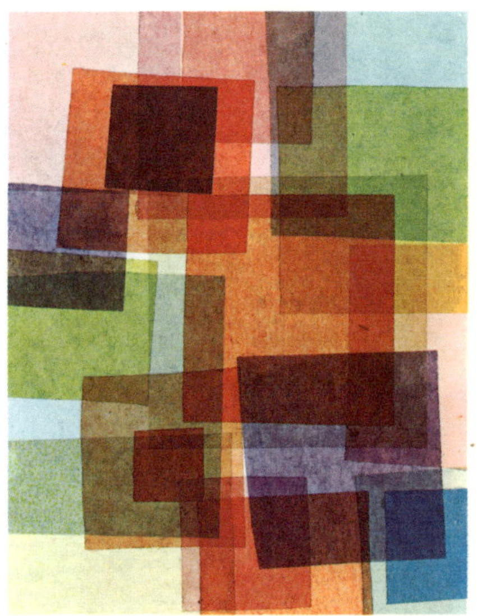

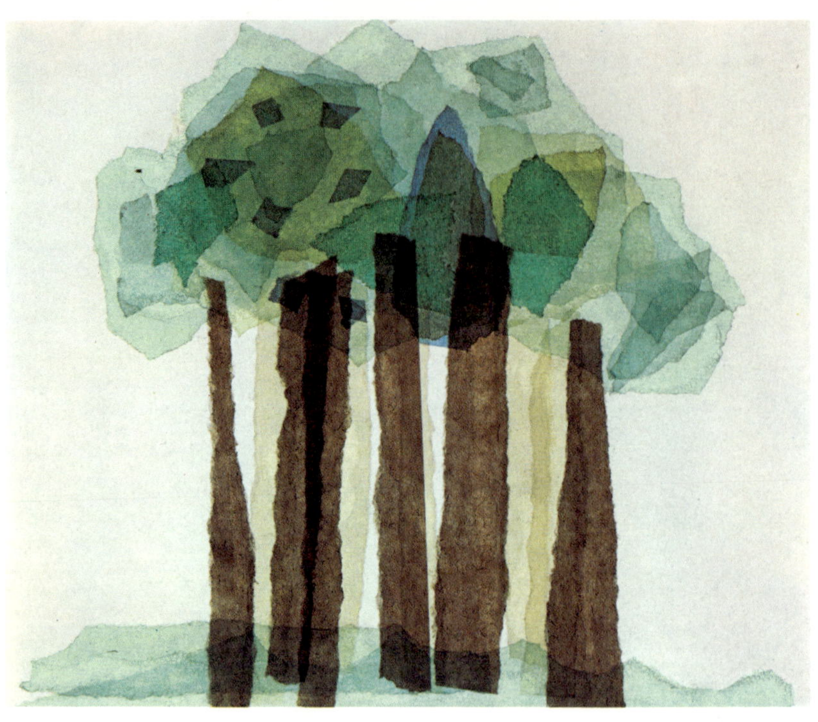

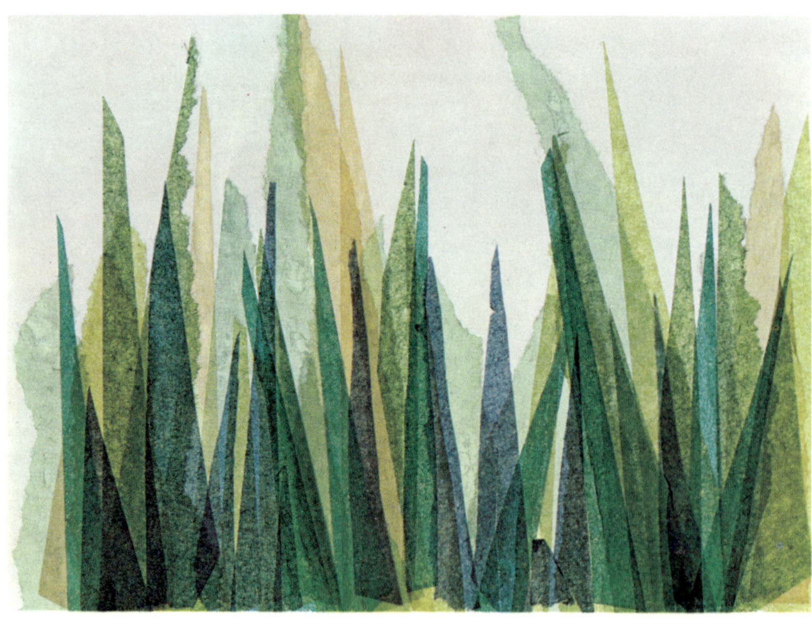

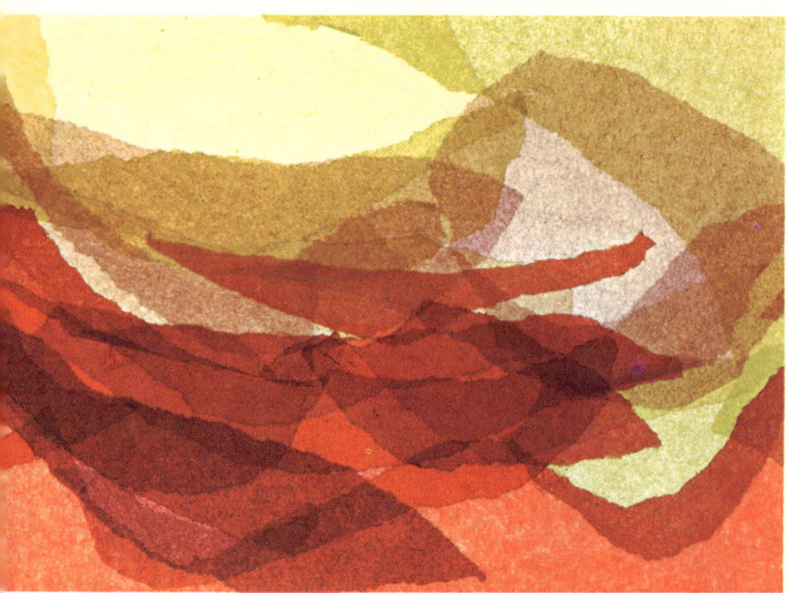

With transparent paper one can gíve a convincing demonstration of the varied range of a single colour family: of green—the colour of the forest and of grass—of the colour of light, or of darkness and mysterious twilight.

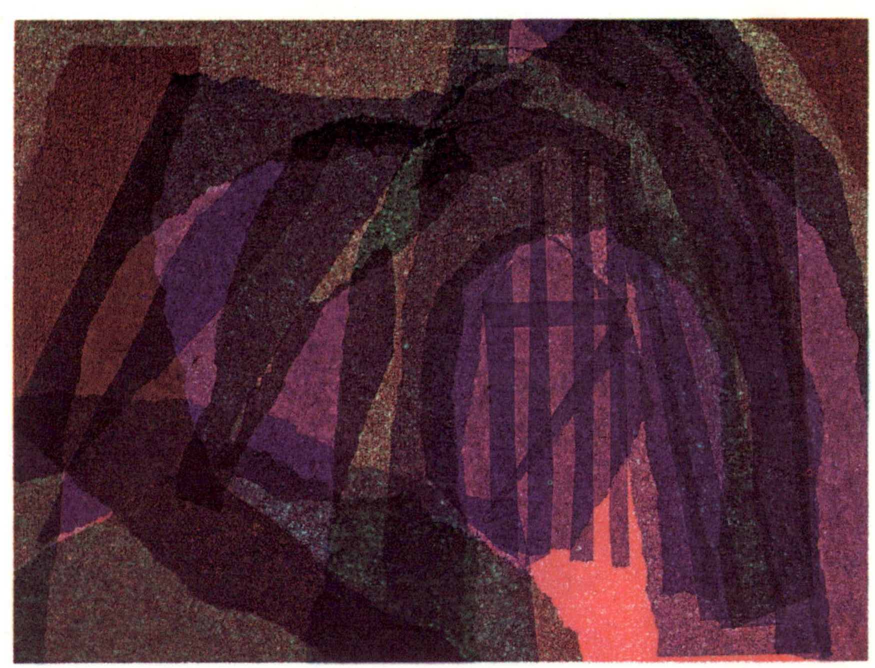

Now we can take a step further and talk about working with a punch. Tiny coloured circles are stamped out with an ordinary office punch machine, or with the type of punch used in leather work. These circular particles can be used to obtain the optical mixture mentioned in the Foreword: a rewarding task for meticulous workers.

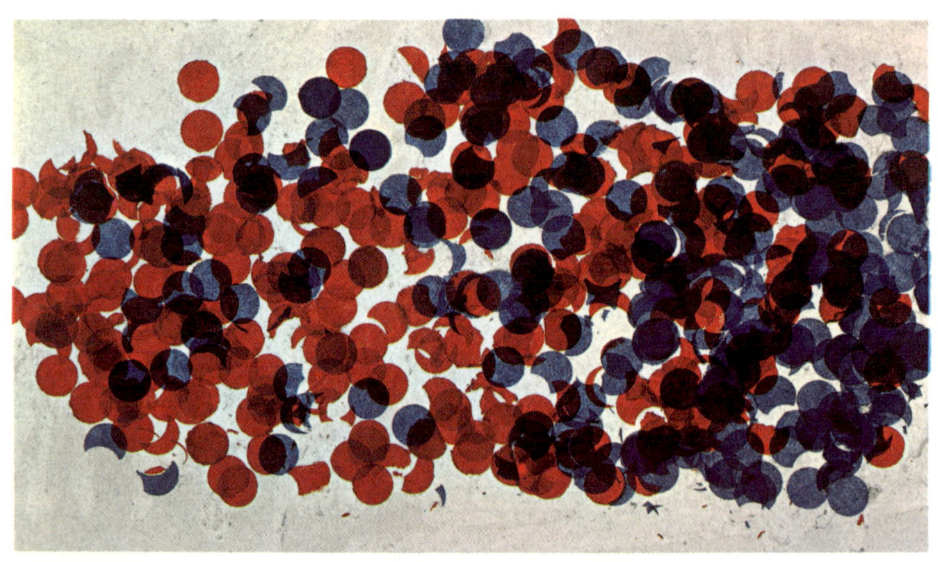

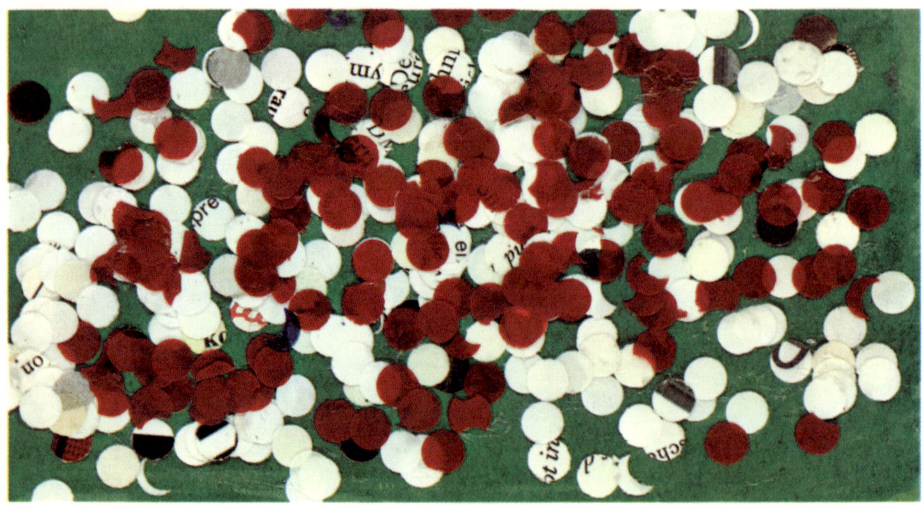

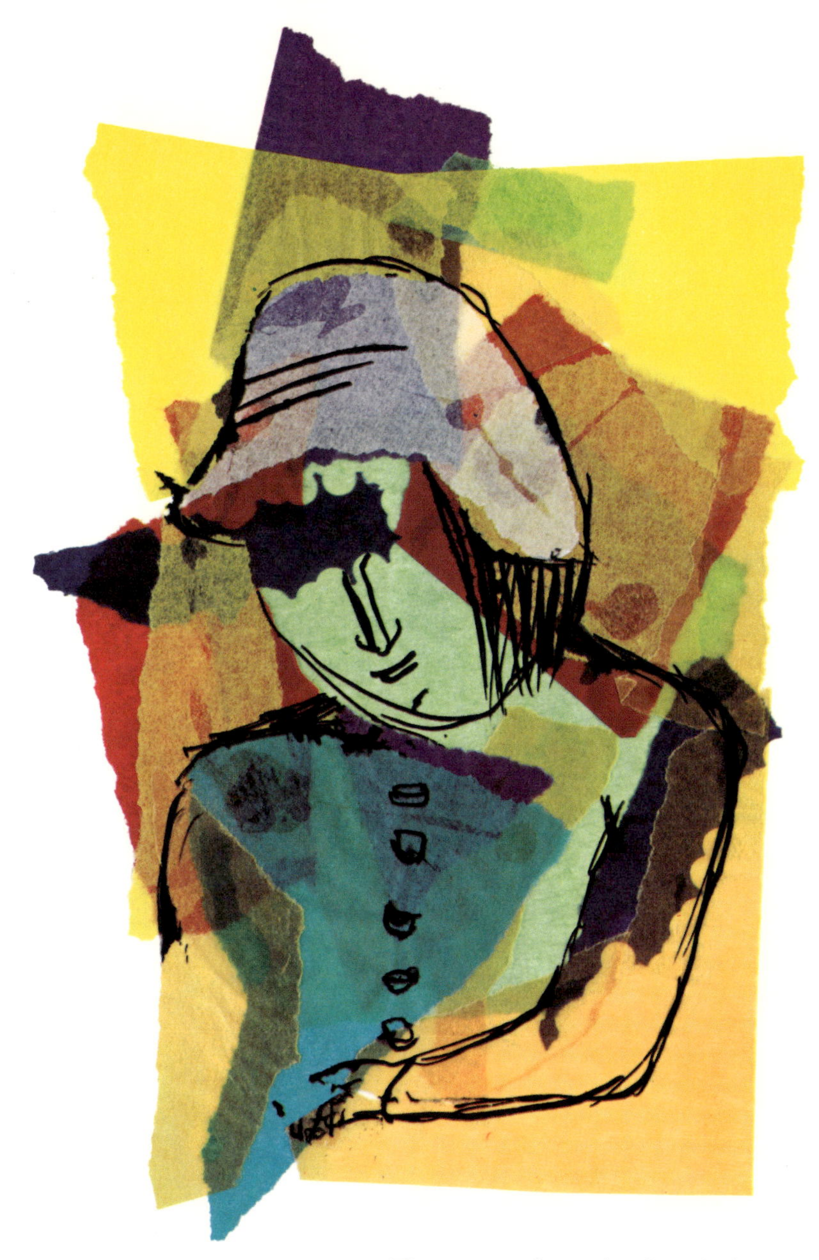

There are also mixed techniques. For instance, pen and ink can be used in a collage

and, of course, in designs in transparent paper.
Collages that are not homogeneous in colouring can be pulled together by spraying them with Chinese ink.

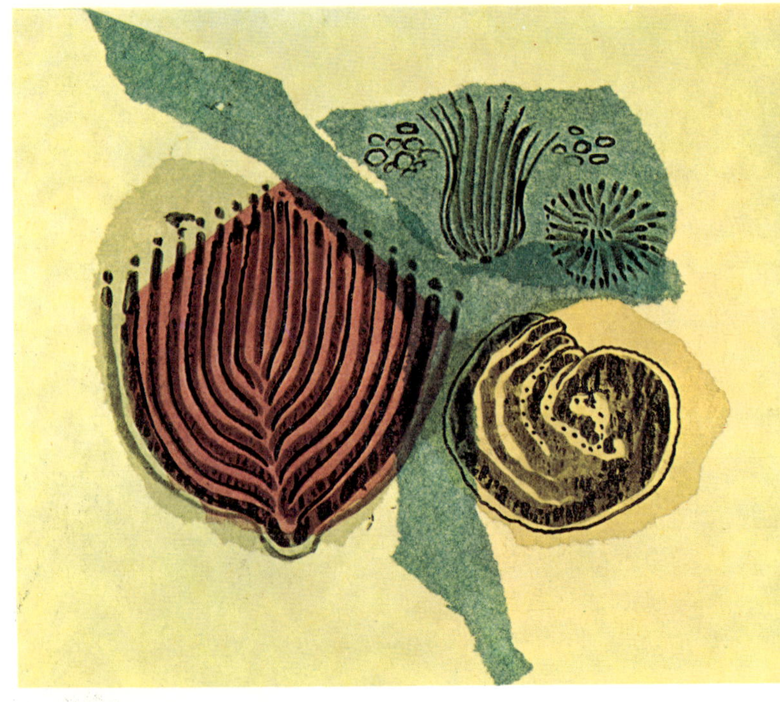

All we have said about the organization of coloured patches applies as well to those produced by punching. These will, however, have less pictorial quality, and be usable only in composing more severe, decorative shapes.

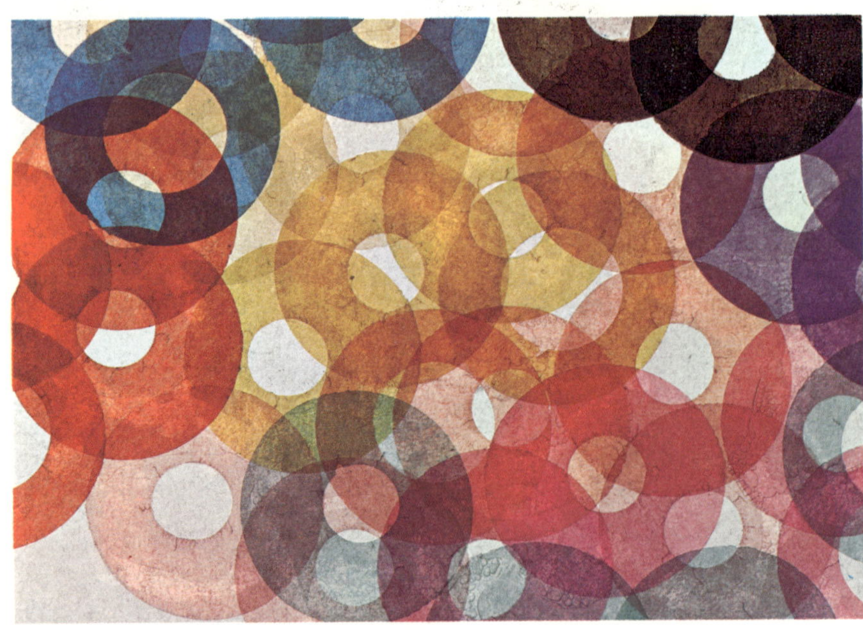

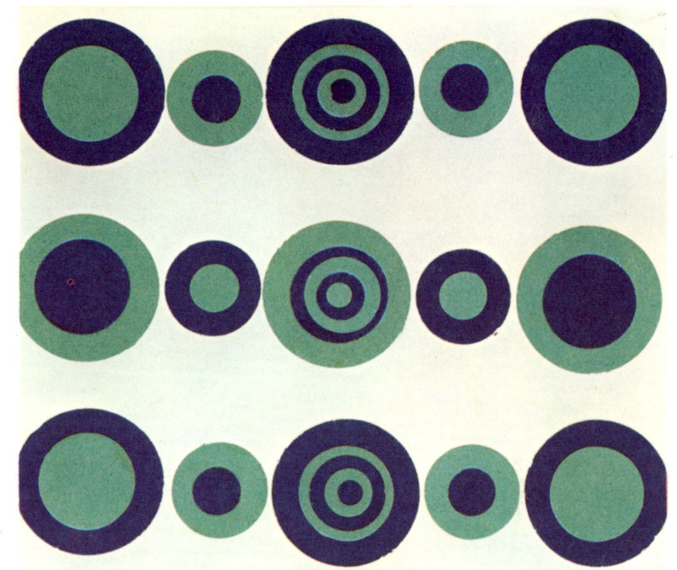

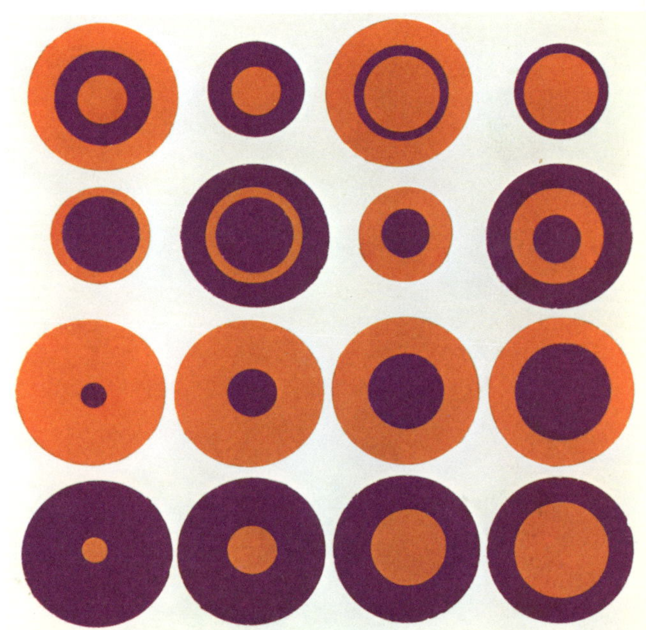

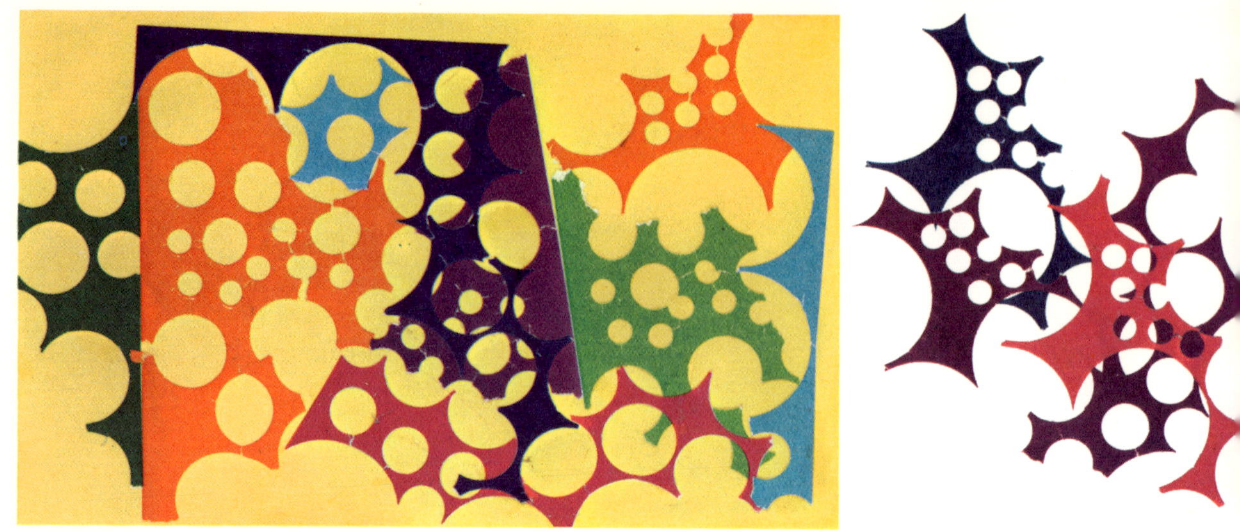

In addition to the punched-out pieces, we can make use of the perforated, original sheet itself, which is laid over a coloured ground, or over another perforated sheet. Positive work can then be added to this.

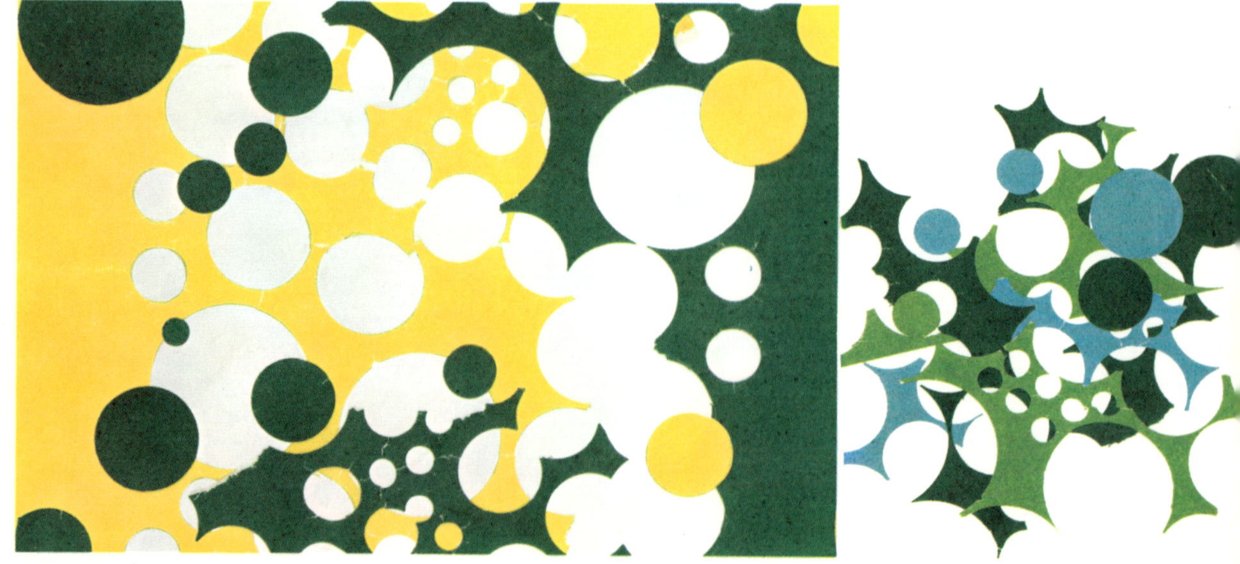

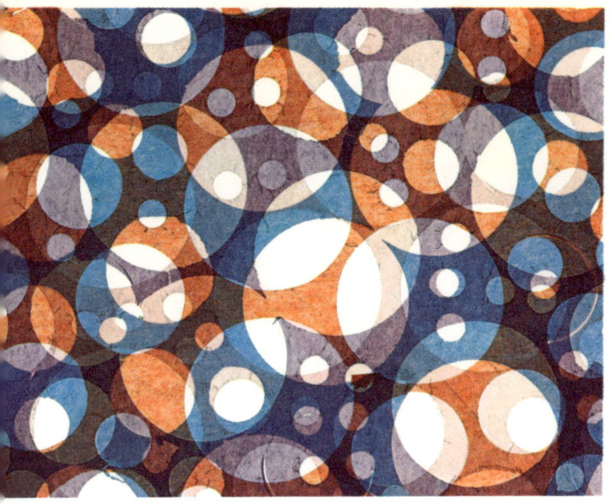

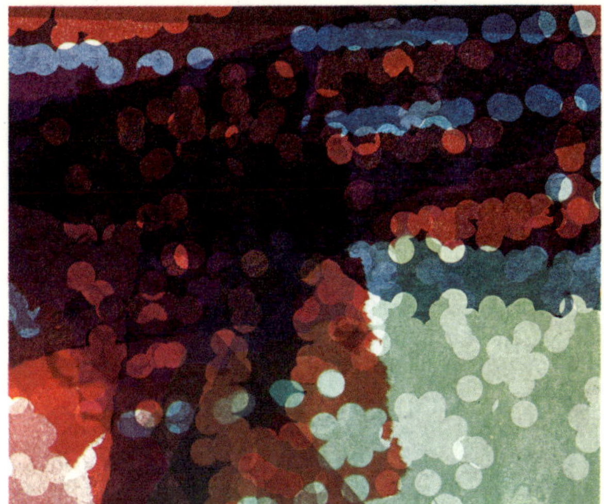

We now have an enormous number of variations at our command, and, as before, further special effects can be obtained with transparent paper.

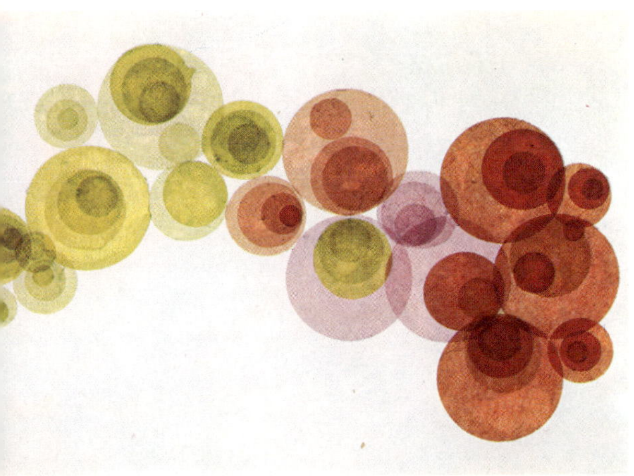

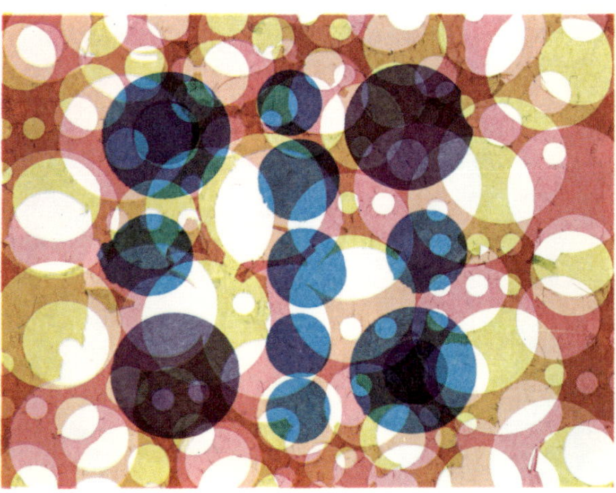

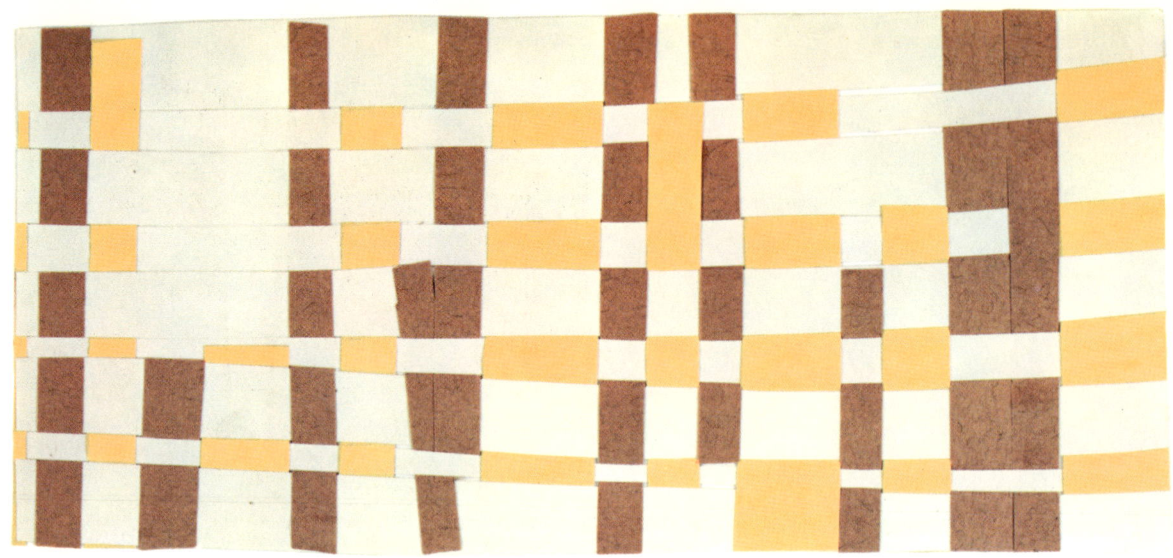

Finally, we must be sure to include woven work, which can be begun in kindergarten.

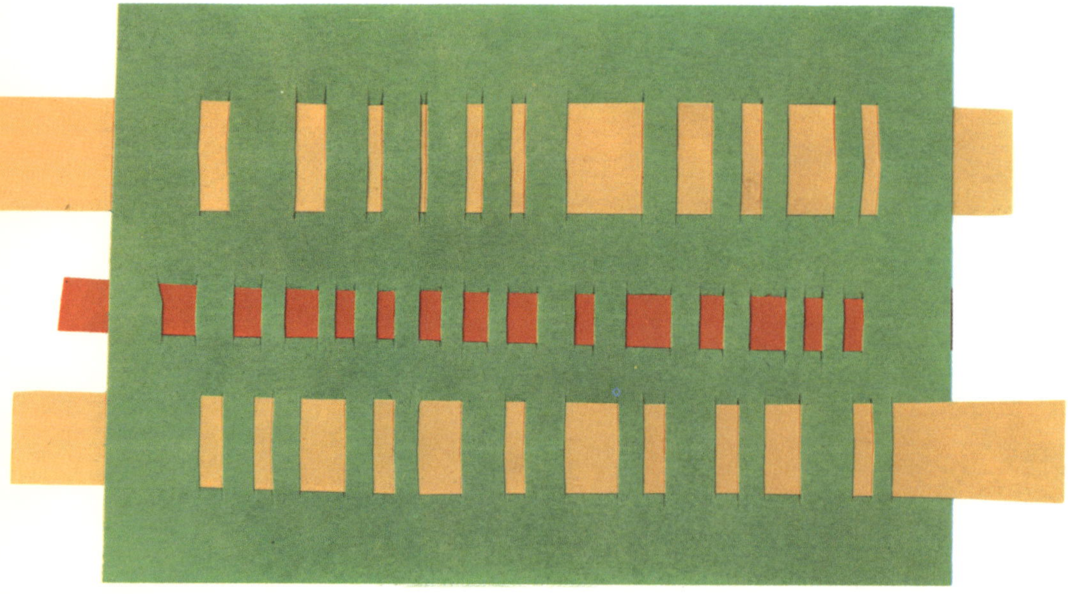

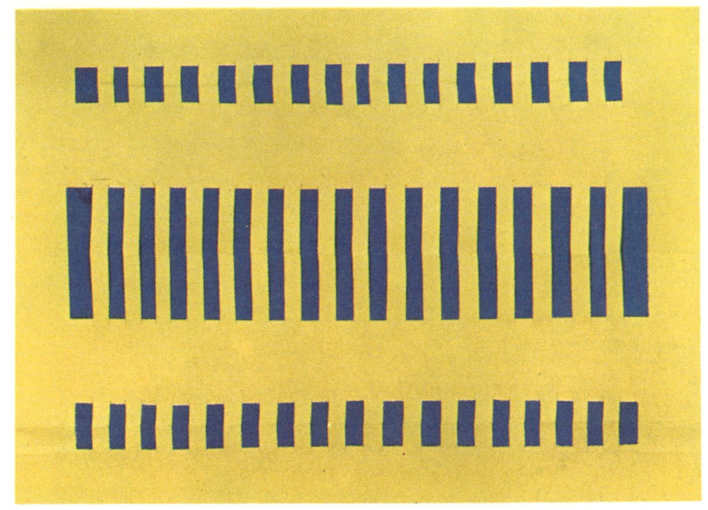

Besides all the two-dimensional techniques, designs in relief can be done well in coloured paper. We begin by cutting slits in the paper at regular or rhythmic intervals, through which coloured strips are then woven. The pictorial effect will vary according to the choice of colour, the length of the slits and the intervals between them.

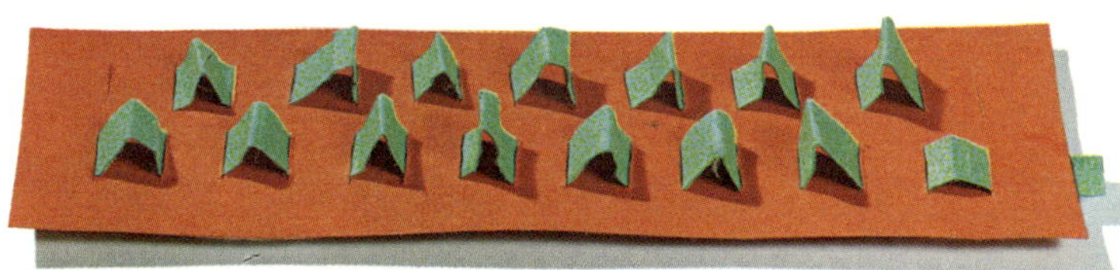

The relief effect is obtained by pulling out the strips and varying the height of the loops.

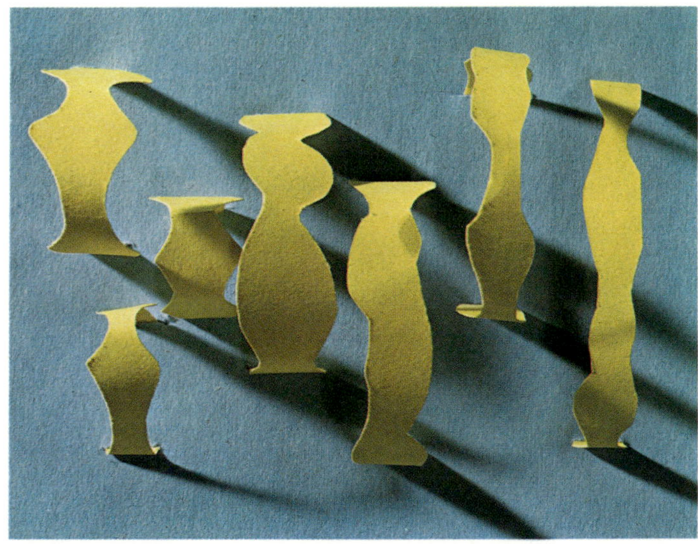

Strips pulled out into loops. Light and shade will then also play a part in the design.

The effect of the uniformly long coloured strips can be enhanced by short, shaped loops which will have the effect of a three-dimensional relief design on a flat surface.

All sorts of interlocking can be used to enliven the woven design in the way of colour, form and plasticity.

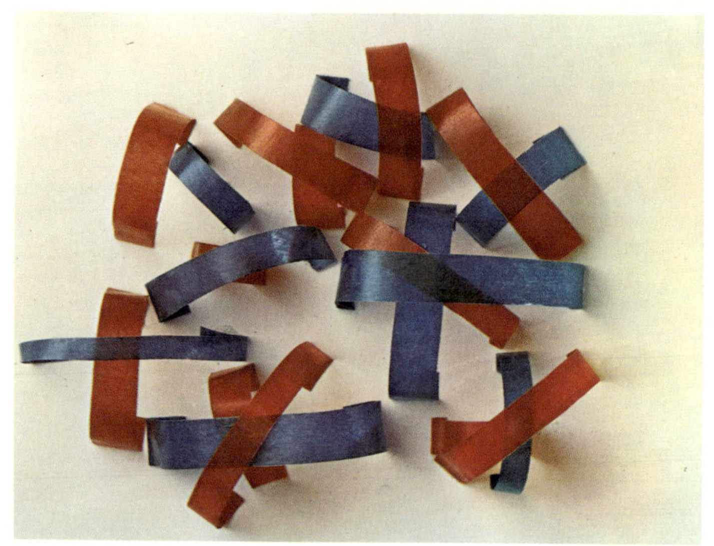

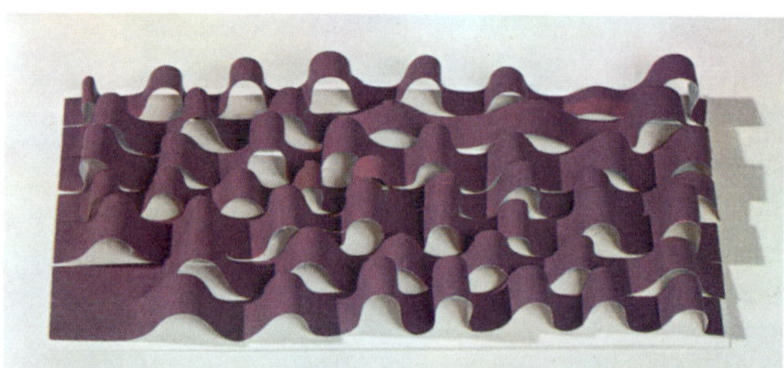

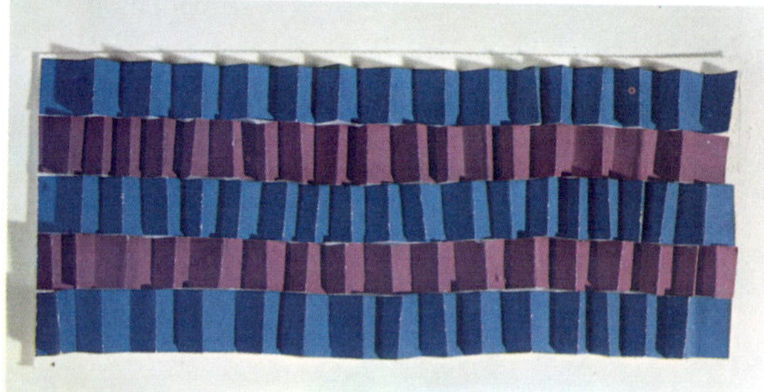

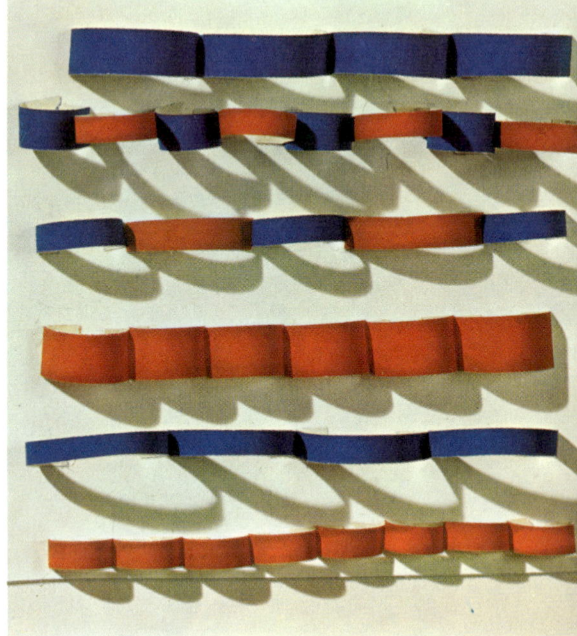

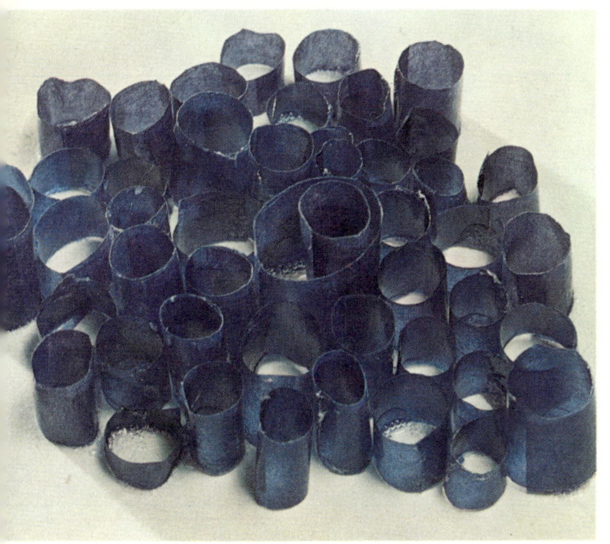

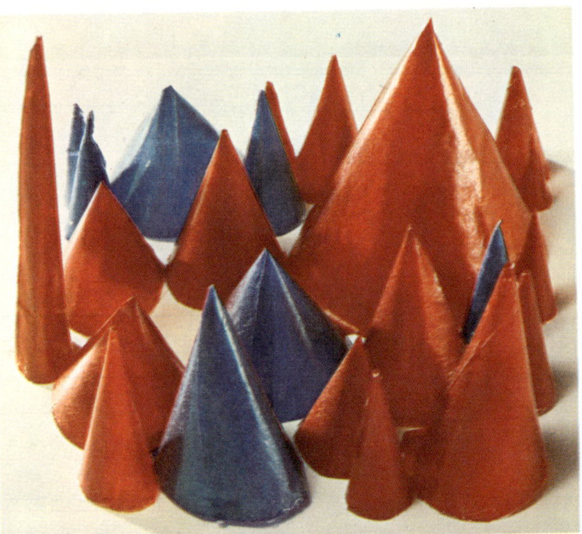

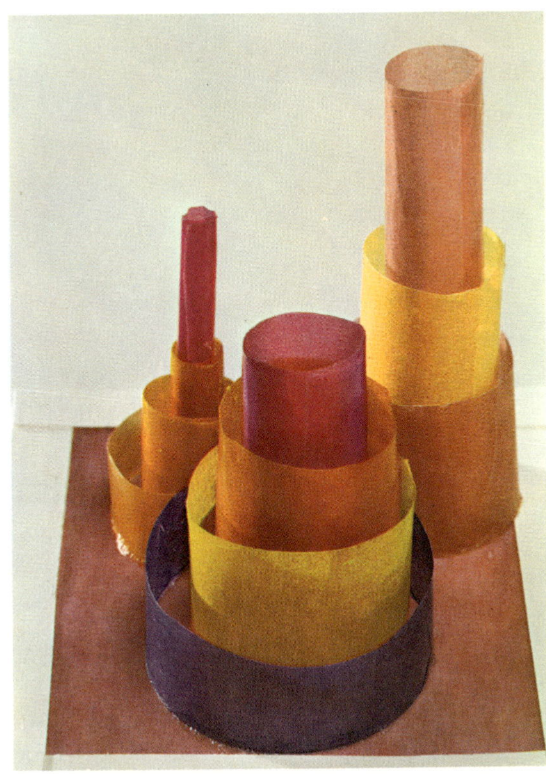

Finally, any strip of paper can be glued together or shaped into a ring, and these attached to the surface, in an almost endless variety of

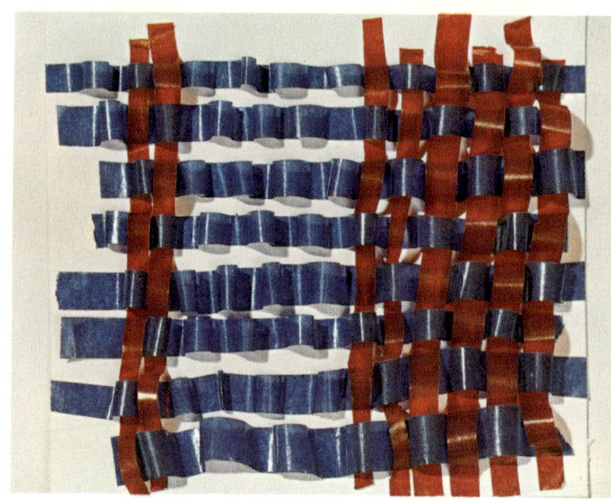

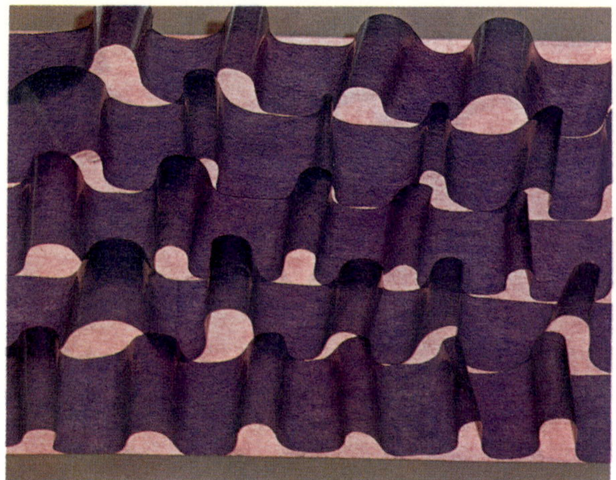

relief compositions.

All of this applies to transparent as well as to opaque paper.

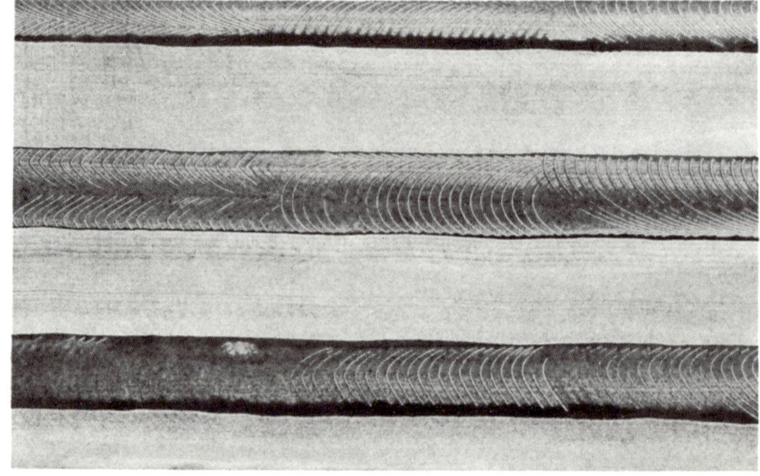

Coloured gummed paper is particularly suitable for binding books and pamphlets. It is perfectly easy to make. Take a large sheet of coated or sized paper (not newsprint), wet it all over and lay it on a table to 'spread'. When paper is wetted it warps and stretches since the fibres swell and become thicker and longer. At the end of five minutes, when it is damp throughout, it can then be smoothed. Spread paste or gum with a paintbrush, but not too thickly or it will crack in drying. The paste itself may be coloured beforehand with drawing inks or paintbox colours.

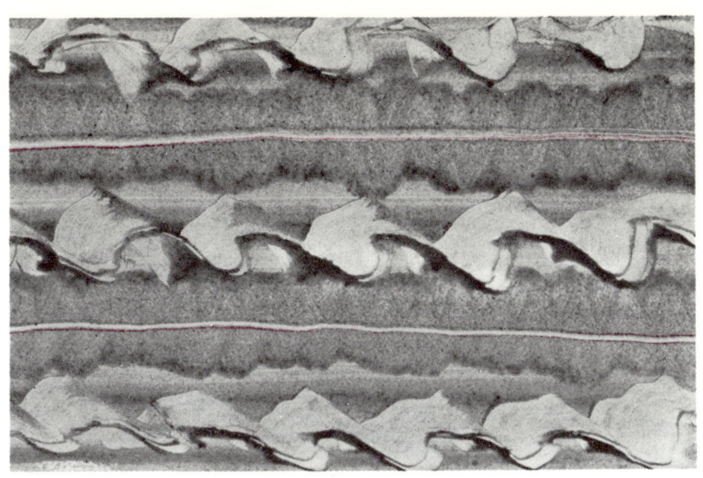

Ordinary opaque paints can be used for embellishing this gummed or painted ground with a brush, and if you like, you can work patterns in it with the handle of the brush, the edge of a piece of cardboard, or a comb.

All kinds of things can be attractively covered with decorative paper, including small boxes and desk accessories.

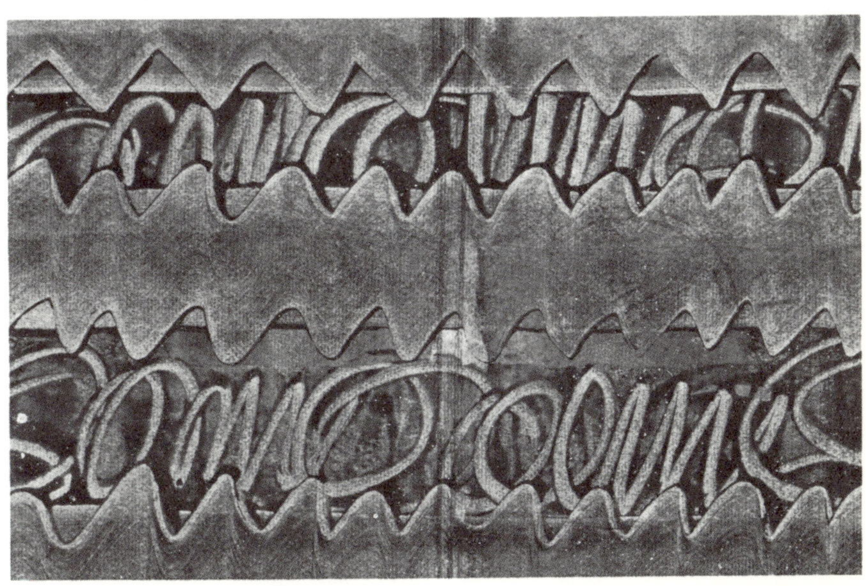

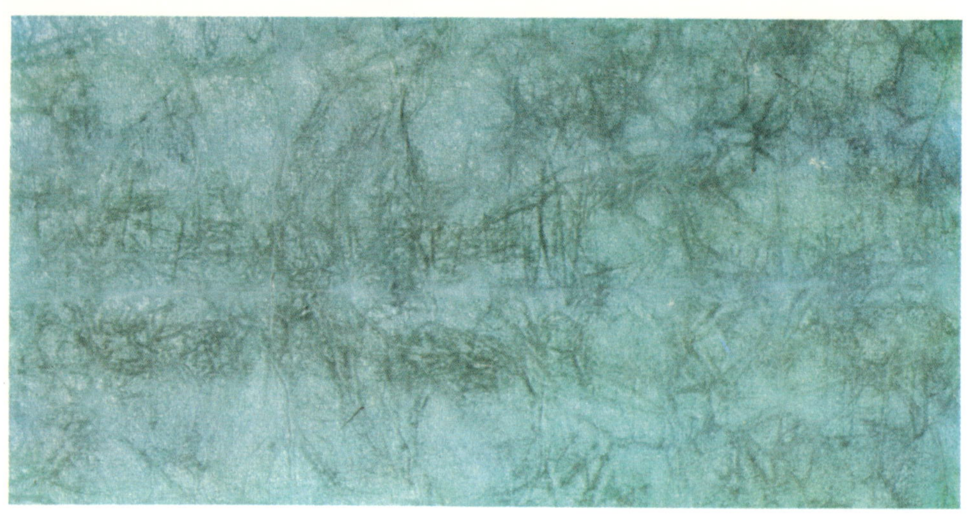

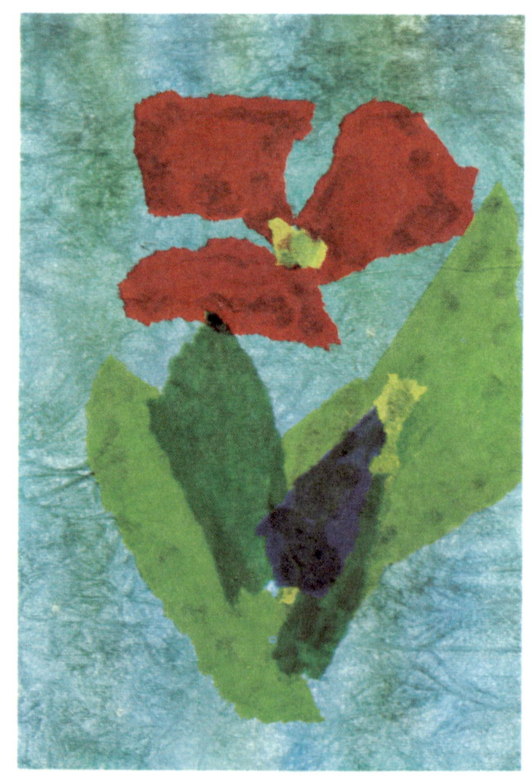

If after all our trouble the pasted paper is a failure, crush it up into a ball with the still wet paint on the inside, and unfold it again. This will crackle the paper, and it can be used as a background for a collage. The uses of decorative paper are inexhaustible. Wonderful effects can be obtained with paste that dries transparent. Transparent coloured inks used in the same way on transparent paper, produce pictorial transparencies that offer a wide scope for individual experiment.

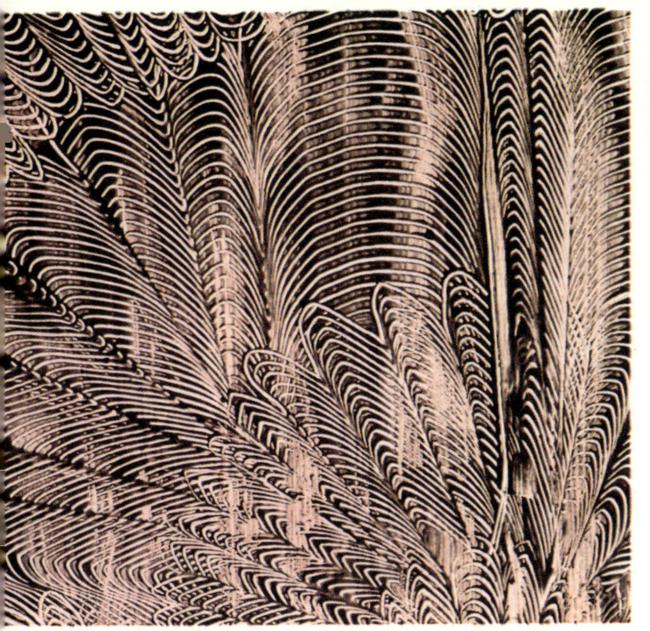

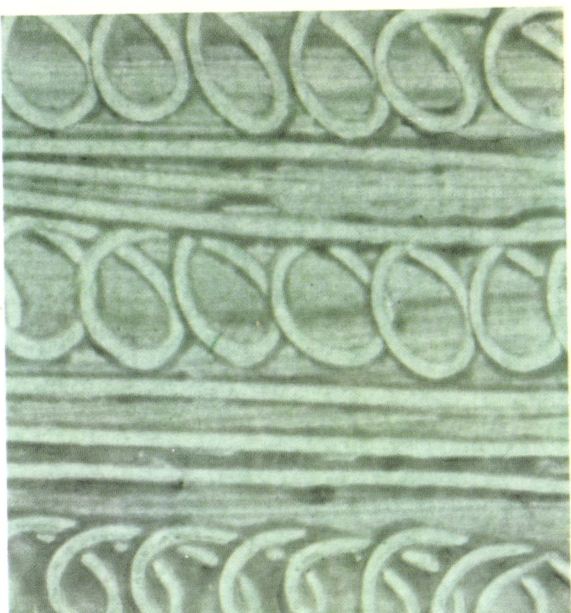

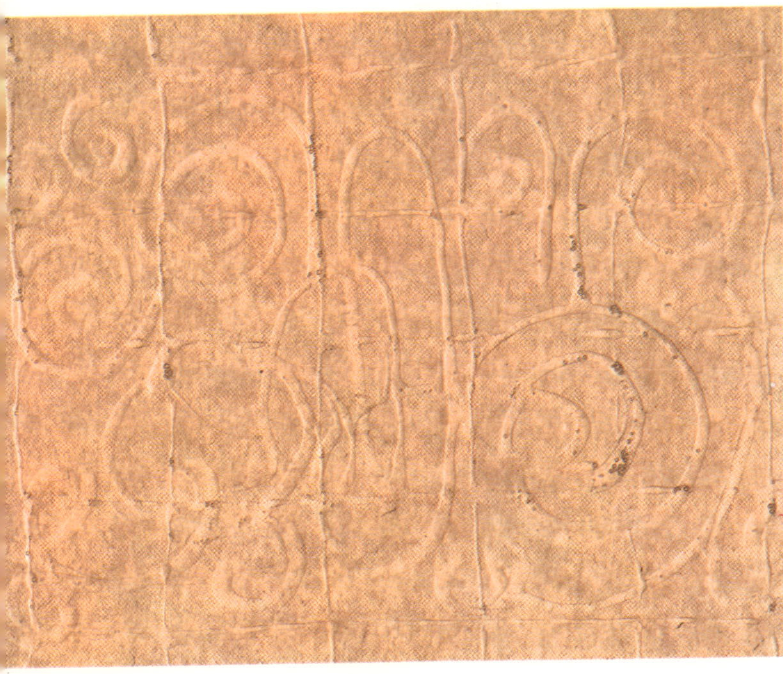

A very simple way of giving transparent paper a structural character is to 'draw' on it with quick-drying cement straight out of the tube.

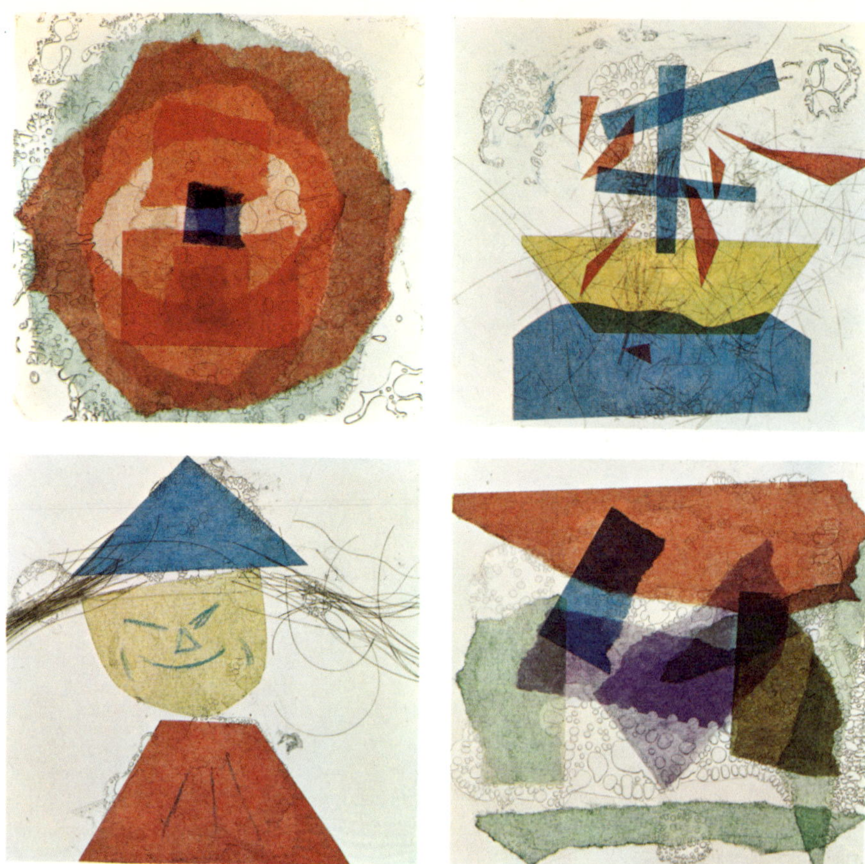

Finally, there is a technique which is not only enjoyable but very instructive, teaching children a great deal about pictorial effectiveness, composition, organization and colour values—results that should be aimed for in any lesson in design.

This consists of making slides with transparent paper. When the design is completed, put a drop of clear-white emulsion on the glass, and cover with the second piece of glass.

This is not by a long way all that can be made with coloured paper, but something must be left for personal experimentation.

Examples of students' designs

We have suggested an abundance of things to tear out, fold and paste down, and a great variety of starting-points for creative design, but every educator knows that techniques are not enough to make children happy painters. Techniques are only the tools, the equipment, with which to express ideas in different forms. Actually, one technique evolves logically out of another; it is the child's inventiveness that counts. The techniques described in the first half of this book must not be taken for recipes to be used indiscriminately. Design should be discussed with the children; they are good inventors, because they still possess the art of play.

Children's play is the form of work best suited to them, and as such it is an undertaking to be taken seriously. The chief task that children are faced with is getting at the secret of the very complex adult world. This work-play helps them towards an understanding of, and an insight into the world around them, which takes very little heed of their needs and desires. Setting children to these technical tasks should not, therefore, be regarded as leading them through a sequence of possible activities. They must be made to be aware of the work as a constructive cycle, and then we shall be helping them to live, leading them towards organized thinking about the outer world and its material resources. Thinking, pondering and working out a coherent idea of the world, are mentally creative capacities we must make sure of developing in them as well. They are fellow-humans and future fellow-citizens. But even a good technique, inventiveness and understanding are not enough for the creation of a picture. The child needs to be given a task. Wanting to paint is as primordial an instinct in children as wanting to help. Wanting to help can atrophy if the child is not allowed to do so, and even if he is, the joy of helping will soon vanish if he is not given a specific task. It is the same with wanting to paint —so much the same, that the urge to paint encounters the same resistance as the urge to help. But if the child is allowed to paint he will want to be assigned a task.

Only the two- to five-year-olds, who are still producing creative symbols out of their own vitality or their private world of childhood, need no challenge beyond that of the material. All other children need a set task to enable them to show what they can do.

They must be given a subject to which they can do justice to in their picture. However, a subject is a very complex affair which must be considered very seriously by the teacher.

In the autumn, in thousands of schools, the usual subject given is 'Autumn as a painter'. A hackneyed subject that can suggest a multitude of things. Analysed didactically, it offers a wealth of pictorial notions which can inspire children to creative work. For instance:

1. 'In the autumn the forest changes colour.' Why? Because the leaves change colour. Thus we have two subjects in one: 'The many-coloured forest' and 'The bright-coloured autumn leaves'. Let us take a step further: 'We lie on our backs on the moss in the wood, and look at the tree tops with their bright-coloured foliage', 'Birds are singing in an autumn tree', 'The animals of the forest meet in the autumn', 'A gale blows through the autumn wood, whipping the branches and twigs and making the leaves fall', 'All the paths are covered with bright leaves'. And as a special subject: 'The forest floor in autumn'. Besides bright leaves there will be big and little stones, fragments of branches, lumps of moss, bits of bark, grass, weeds and berries.

2. 'Autumn is harvest time.' Who does the harvesting? The farmer, the neighbours, and even children. What is harvested? Apples, pears, plums, rye, wheat, oats, hay, all sorts of vegetables in the fields.
Themes can be drawn from all of these:
'Our neighbour harvests his fruit.'
'We pick apples from the tree.'
'The big fruit farm.'
'We eat lunch after our work, surrounded by baskets of fruit.'
'The harvester is driven through the ryefield.'
'The farm labourers rest among the sheaves.'
'Potato harvest.'
'We sit round the fire roasting potatoes.'

3. 'Mother makes plum jam.'
'We help Mother with the bottling.'
'We carry the preserves down to the cellar.'
'The shelves in the cellar are chock-full of preserves.'
'We put the apples and pears on long shelves.'

4. 'School begins in the autumn.'
'Parents bring young children to school.'
'The children stand at the school

door with their new school bags.'
'All the things I have in my bag.'
'Our teacher photographed us like this.'

5. We have come back from the holidays, remembering all the things that happened.
'We bathed in the sea.'
'At the swimming pool.'
'How the beach looked from our window.'
'We went out to sea in a rowing-boat.'
'We saw the big ships in the harbour.'

6. Winter is approaching.
'There is frost over all the hedges.'
'Landscape in autumn mist.'
'Flight of birds across the autumn sky.'

The scope of the subject, 'It's autumn now', is thus opened wide, and given a little more effort can go wider still. And how little, by comparison, can be got out of 'Autumn as a painter'. This is the benefit of analysis; it forces one to think things out.

But further consideration will be needed. What technique, and what materials will be best suited to these various subjects? In a sense they could all be treated in any of the techniques and materials we have described. But one or other of these may be found most suitable—perhaps done in coloured paper—and all this must also be decided on. Besides, not every subject is suited to every child. A 'literary' subject will present different difficulties to different ages, and on the 'technical' side does this as well. The teacher must consider the ability of the class to treat the subject in the light of previous work and its degree of acquired knowledge.

Then comes the art teacher's primary concern: What is our chief *aim* at the moment? What must the children learn next? What element of pictorial design must they be helped to grasp now?

Designing in coloured paper affords opportunities for all sorts of preparatory tasks. The theme chosen can help the pupil to express the tension between light and dark, big and little, bright and dull, heavy and light, or to harmonize colours by a uniform veiling of grey, to differentiate between shades of a single colour, and the use of related and of contrasting colours. It will also afford exercises in planning colour areas, in mixing colours and in over-all organization.

All this must be kept in mind if a passively artistic project is to lead to an actively artistic education. Considering a theme for its educational value will help the teacher to plan the steps he must take, the best method by which to proceed. For instance:

1. What does the main theme (of the week, month or term?) suggest in the way of developing subsidiary ones? We can select one pictorial aspect of autumn: 'A gale blows through the autumn wood.'

2. This secondary subject can then be analysed in depth for its pictorial possibilities: 'The trees sway in the wind. Branches and leaves are thrashing about. Leaves are torn off and fly through the air. The leaves that lie thickly on the ground are whirled high in the air. They collect in crevices and corners. Gradually the trees become bare. They stand almost black against the sky. The slender, young trees are swept hardest by the wind. Sometimes the gale breaks off branches from the tall, old trees, and they fall with a crash to the ground. Often whole trees are uprooted. The storm may be accompanied by thunder and showers of rain or hail. Then the landscape grows dark, lighted up now and then by bright flashes of lightning.'

All this wealth of content invites pictorial representation. What technique does it suggest?

3. Many techniques are possible:
Pen and ink drawing.
Brush drawing.
'Wet-on-wet' painting.
Cardboard printing.
Finger painting.
Wax-crayon painting.
Scratch technique.
Monotype.
Colour sgraffito.
Collage or décollage.
Cut and torn coloured paper, and so on.

Let us opt for coloured paper for the moment. We must first decide whether to tear the paper or to cut it. Tearing would be best suited to the 'gale'. If we want a decorative effect, mono-coloured, bought paper will be best; but if we want form and colour to bring out the dynamic character of our storm picture, our home-made, unevenly coloured paper will prove most effective. It would also be a good idea to use transparent paper, to suggest the dull, misty atmosphere of that sort of day.

4. When we have chosen our subject and technique, we must ask ourselves, 'What has this task to teach us from the point of view of art? Shall we work in black, white and grey, to help the children to seek as many shades of grey as possible, and to distinguish between them? Or in brown, so that they realize the greater wealth of

shades in brown than in grey? Or plan to get the effects of light and dark, the play of contrasting colours, or the alternation between large patches of colour and graphic structure? Even with this minimal restriction, the correct coloured paper must be procured or selected.

5. One question remains: What among all the foregoing are we finally to present to the children? The subject may be quite suitable, but the technique too difficult, or a pictorial representation of the subject may be beyond their mental development. On the other hand, children should not be given a subject they are too old for, nor a technique that will bore them because it is already too familiar.

Children of 6 to 8 will be content with tearing shapes and pasting them in the right places, but we must decide whether trunks, branches and twigs are to be torn separately and then built up (additive technique), or whether the trees are to be torn out all in one piece. At this early stage the additive process is probably the best. They can select the colours themselves—bright ones, most likely—although the teacher should be at hand to advise against too garish a medley.

Those from 9 to 11 will expect something more in the way of subject and technique. They have a feeling for movement, and may show a considerable degree of emotional 'engagement' and a capacity for imaginative self-expression.

Children of 12 to 15 have entered the critical phase. They want to be less childish; and they are inclined to consider a great many things as childish. Technical difficulties often present a sporting stimulus. They can grasp the idea of formal organization of colour and form. They are more sensitive than they choose to appear. All this must be reckoned with. Of course every teacher knows best what his pupils are like, what they can do, and what they urgently need.

The following pages show a collection of school work done with coloured paper.

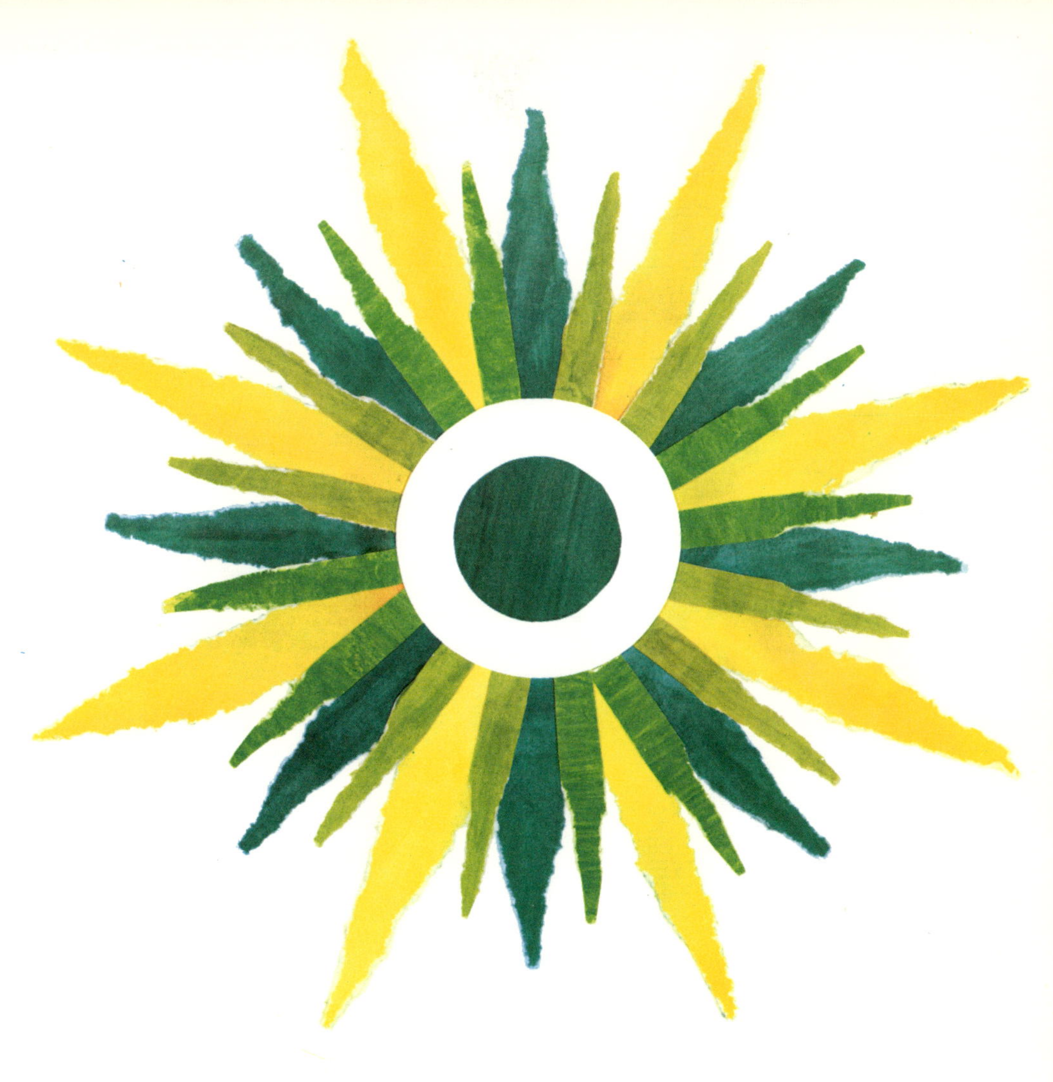

'Central organization.' Collage of hand-coloured paper (girl of 14). For description of technique, see p. 10.

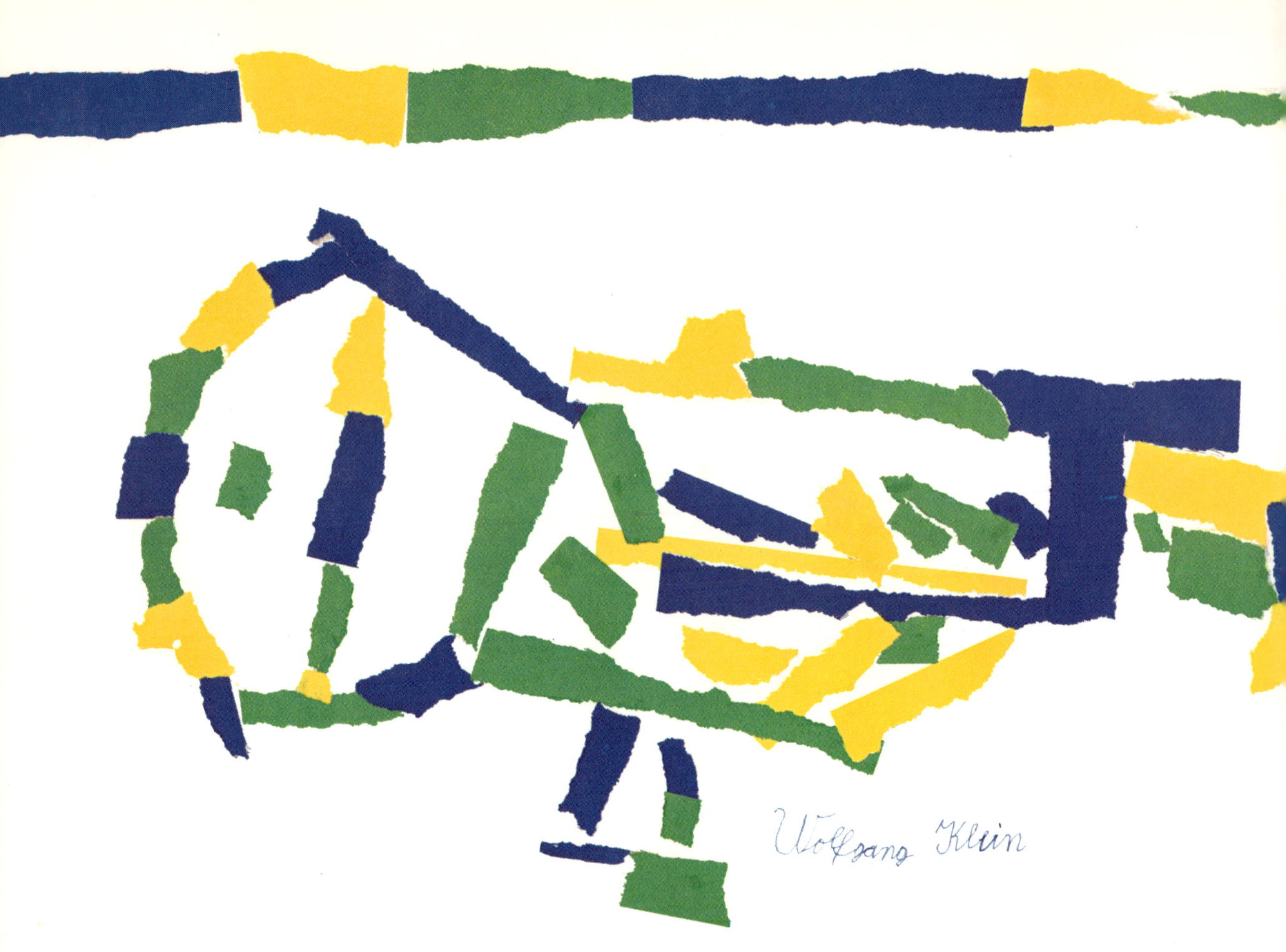

'My pet bird.' The colours were restricted to blue, green and yellow. The way in which the boy has organized the bright feathers into outlines is characteristic (boy of 6). For technique, see pp. 9–11.

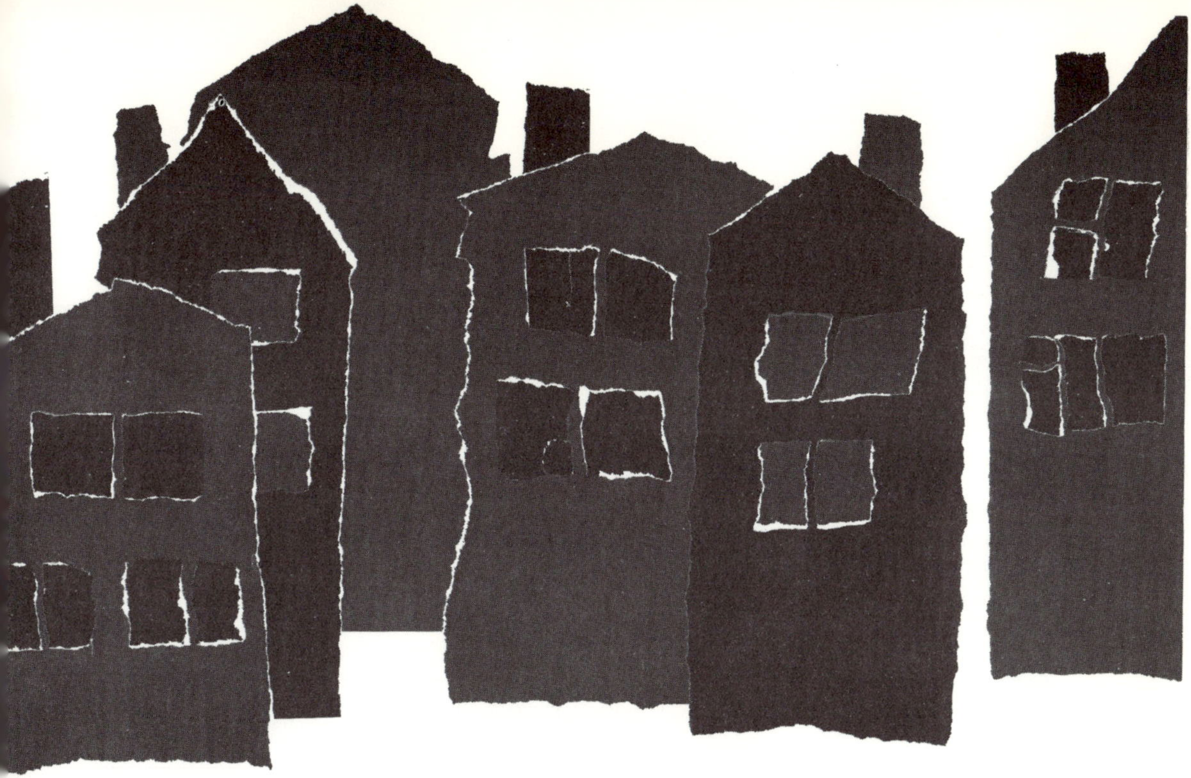

'Black and grey town.' Collage. For technique, see p. 21.

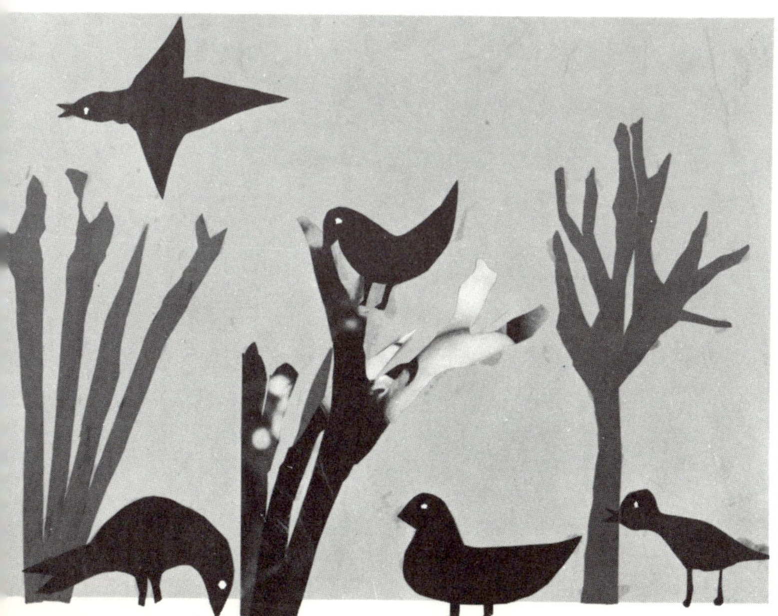

'Birds in winter' (girl of 12). For technique, see p. 21.

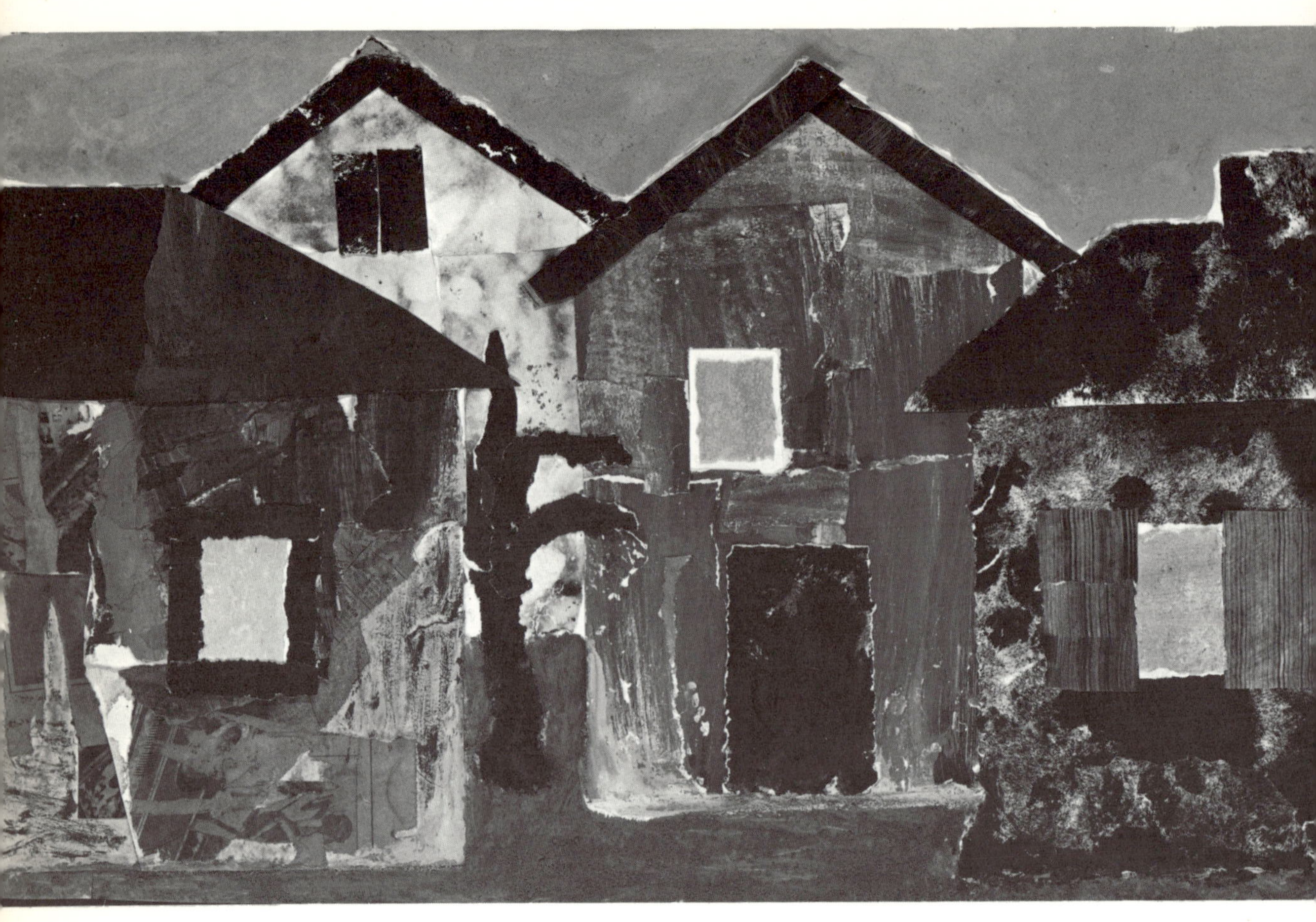

Above:
'Grey town.' Collage (girl, 16). Cut and torn hand-coloured paper and newspaper. Sand was worked into some of the paint. For technique, see p. 21.

Right:
'Cat in a grey cellar.' Collage (boy, 9). Newspaper on hand-coloured paper.

'The grey hen.' Collage. Cut-out, hand-painted paper. For technique see pp. 9–11.

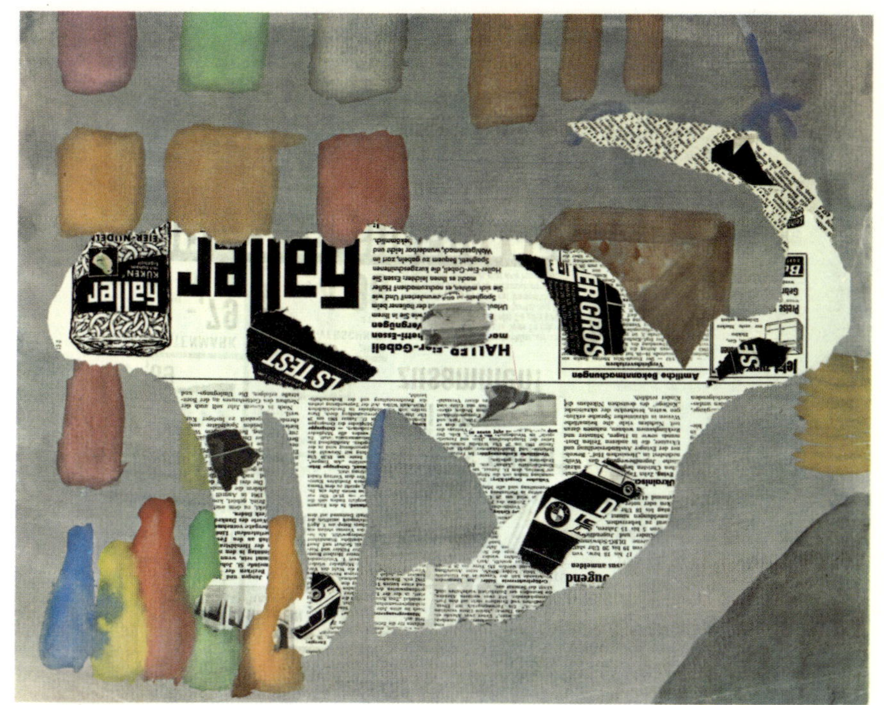

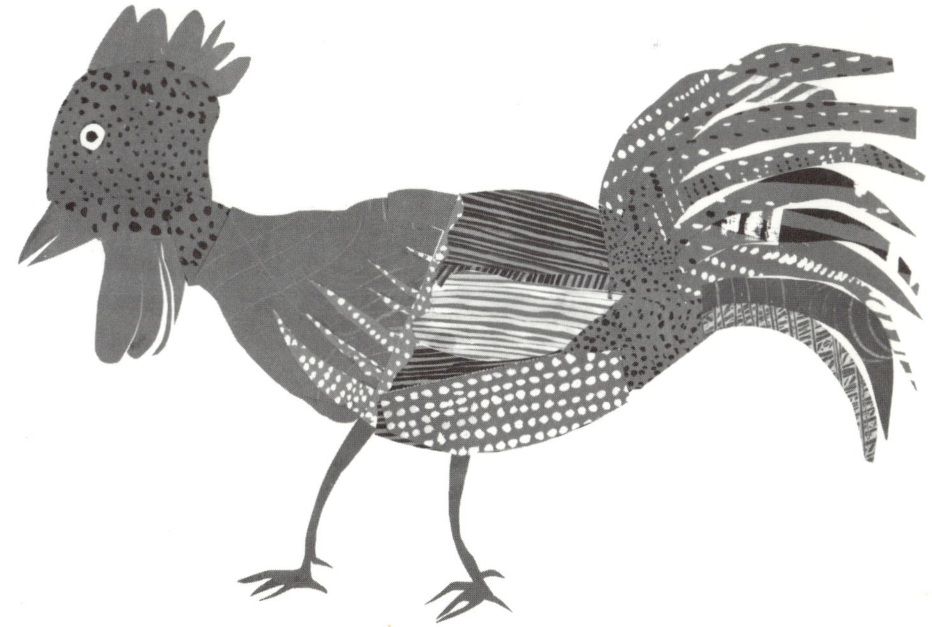

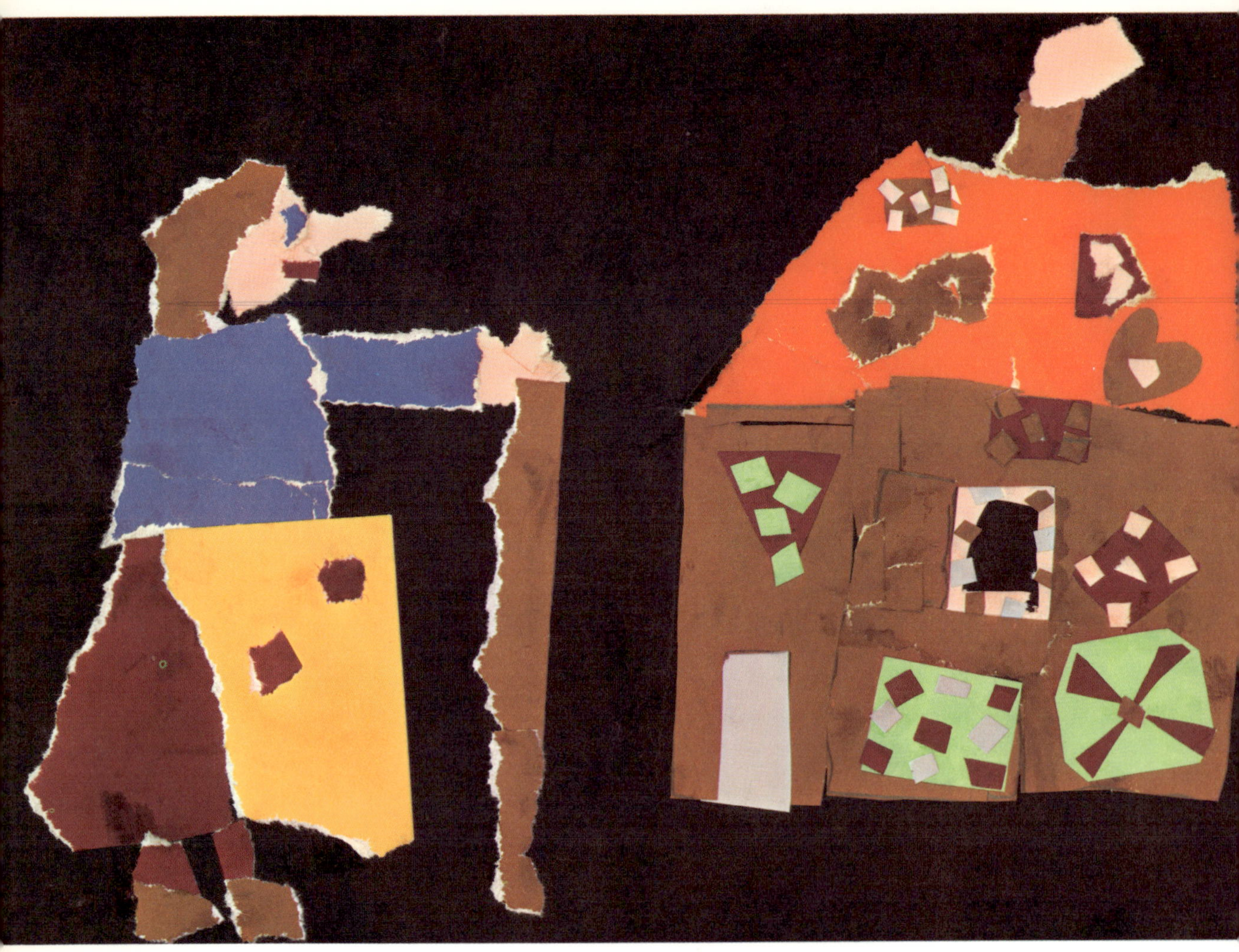

Above:
'The witch standing in front of her house.' Gummed coloured paper, torn and cut (girl, 8). For technique, see p. 21.

Right:
'Colour composition with scraps of coloured paper.' Two methods of organizing a surface in mosaic style. The upper design is a structural composition, the lower one a harmonizing of small, scattered fragments. For technique, see pp. 9–11.

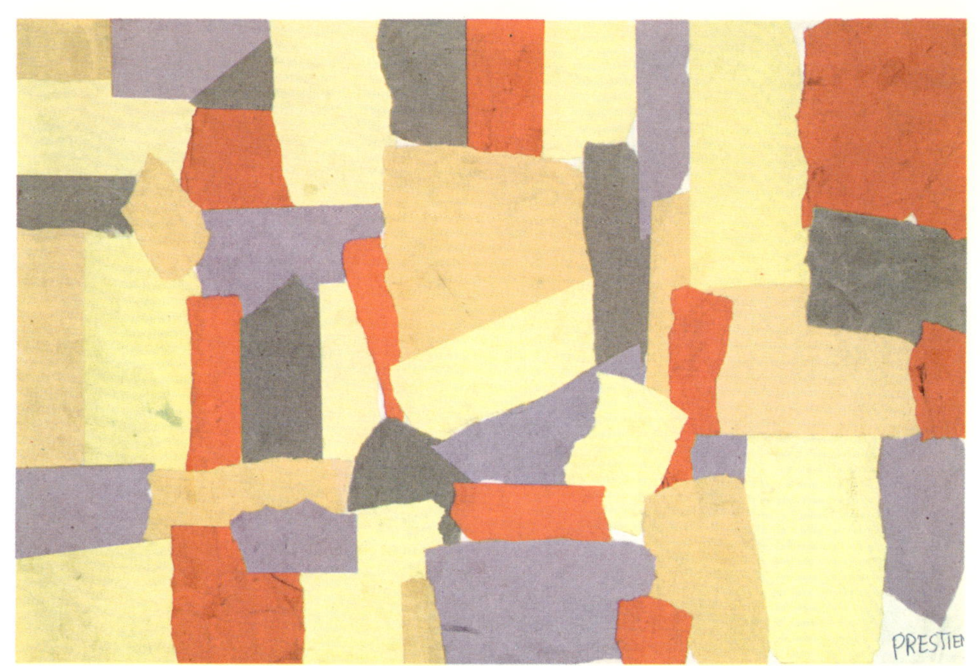
PRESTIEN

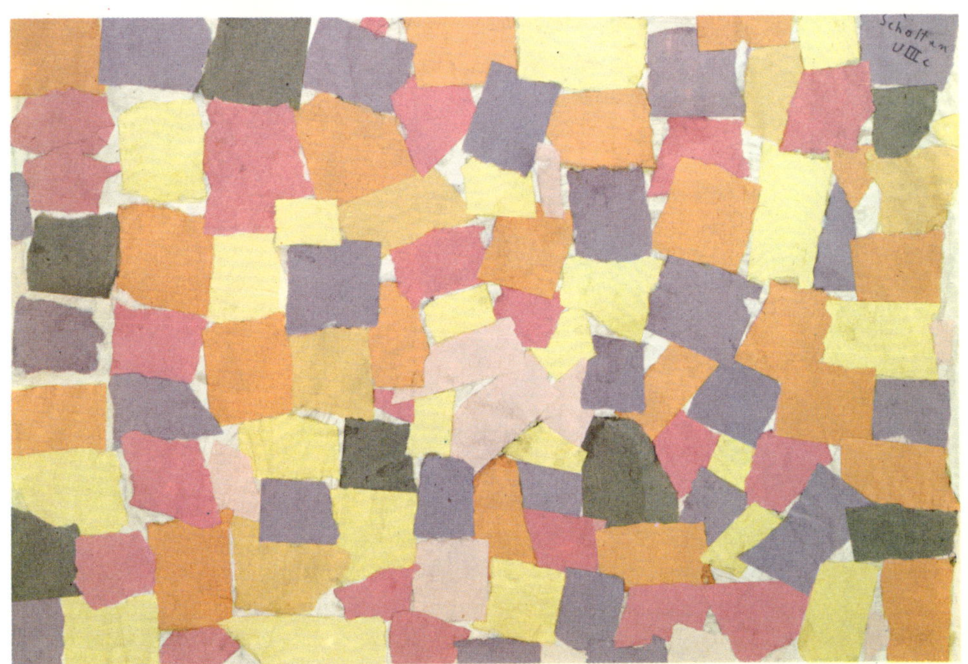
Scholten
UIIIc

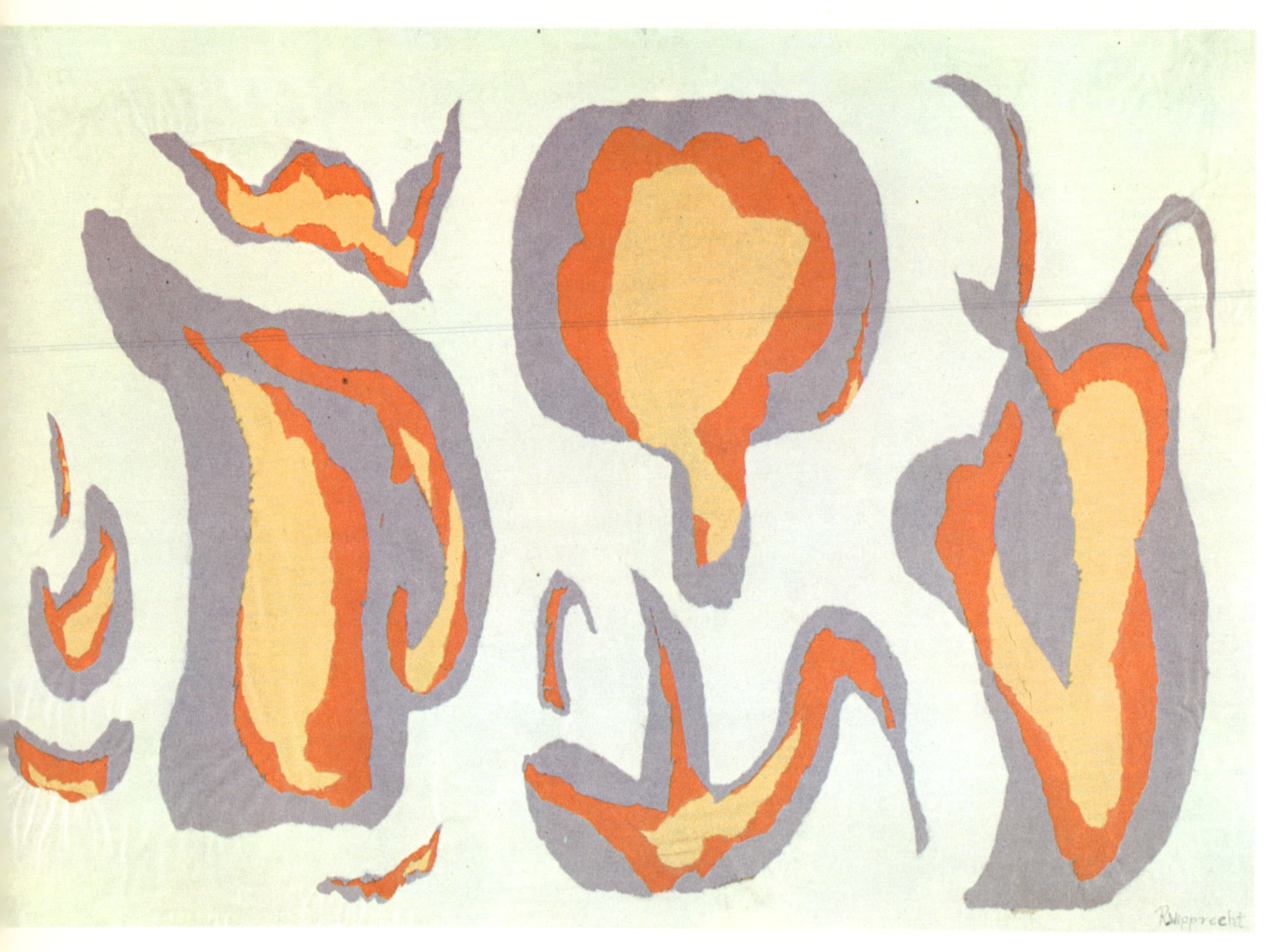

Above:
Collage. Four layers of colour (boy, 14). For technique, see pp. 18–22.

Right:
'Lattice collage,' (group work by five boys of 11). Each boy contributed a 'lattice'. The work was produced by shifting these about, under discussion, then pasting them down.

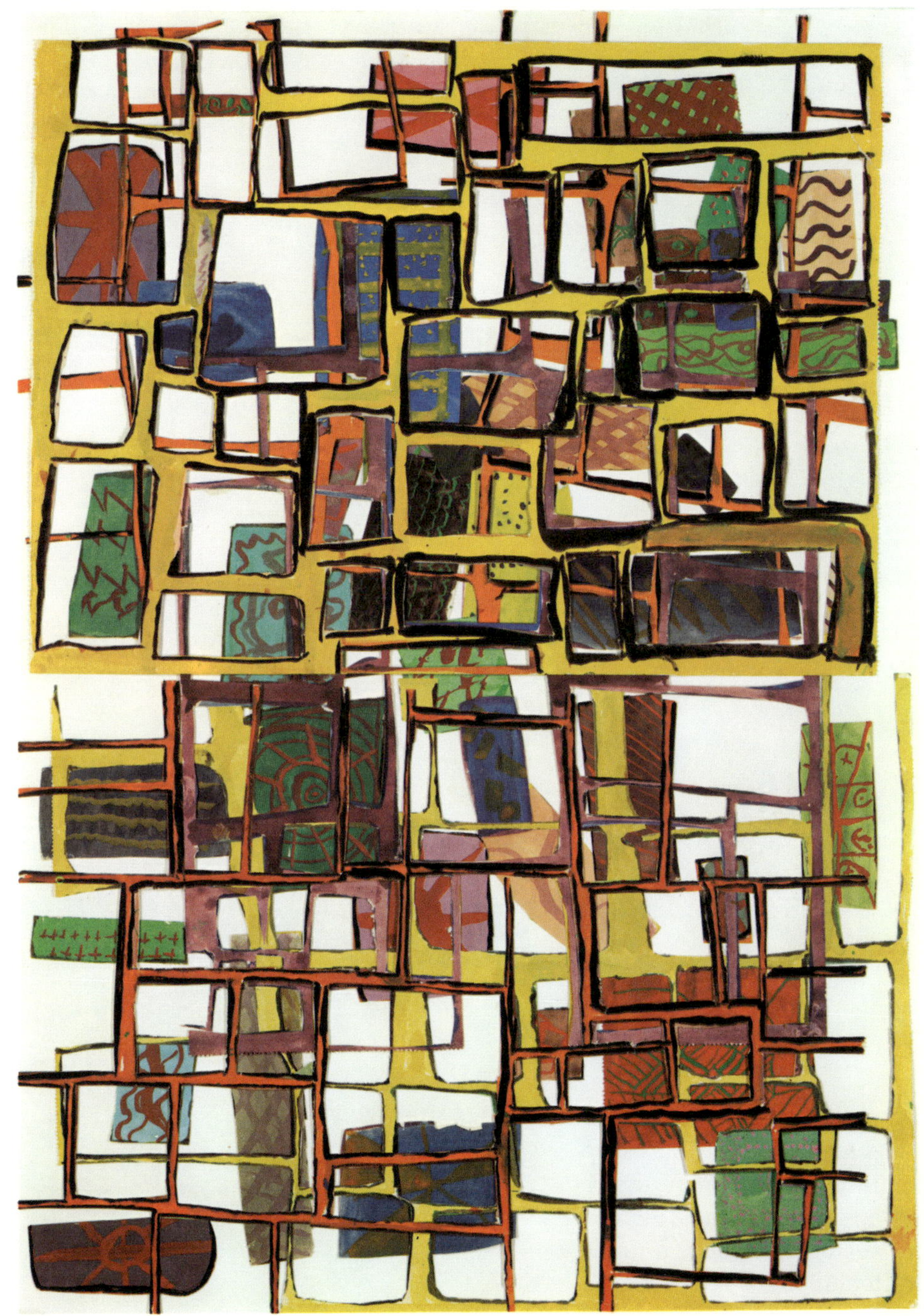

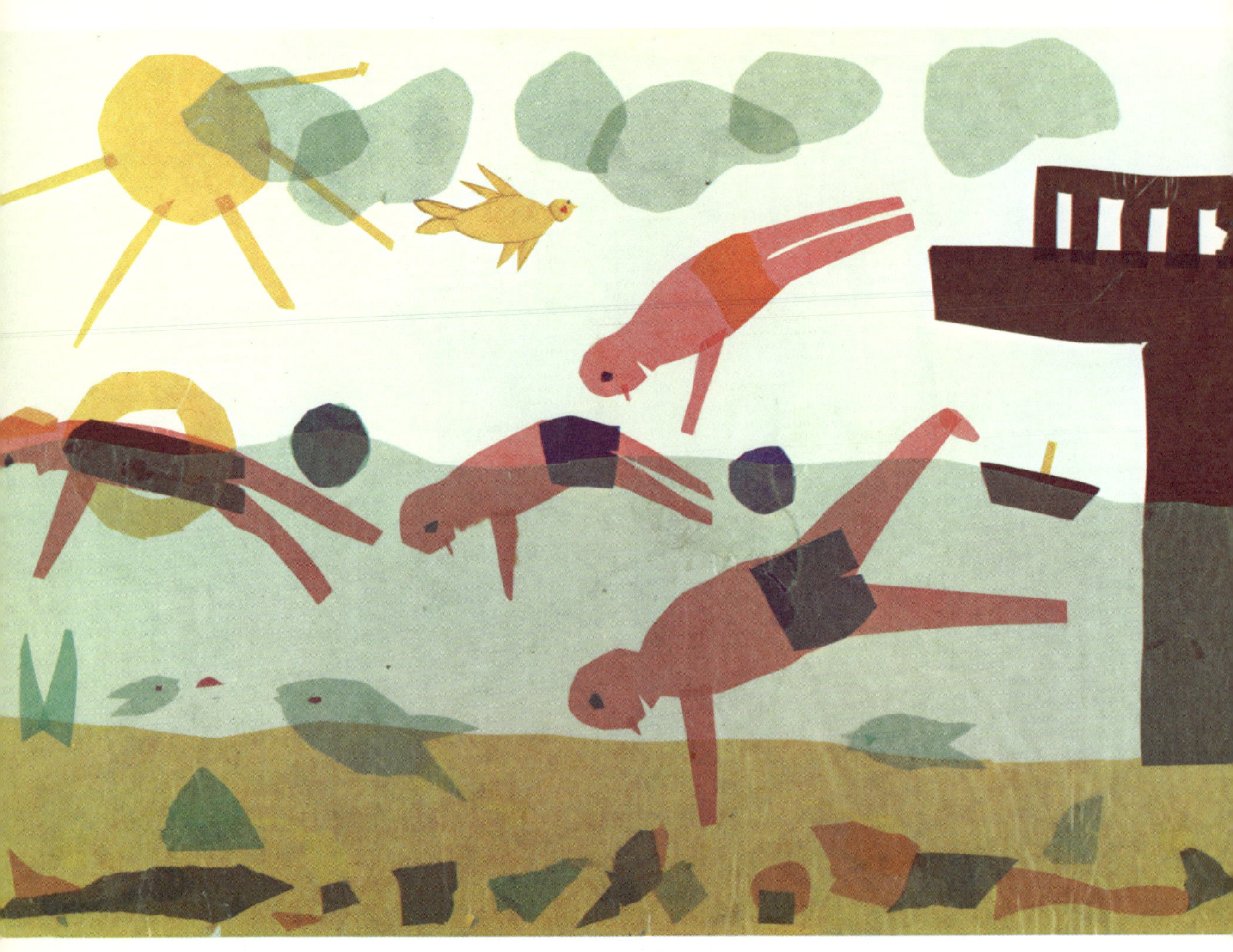

'At the swimming pool.' Cut out of transparent paper. This is an example of the 'harmonizing' effect of transparent paper. The men can be seen swimming underwater. For technique, see p. 23.

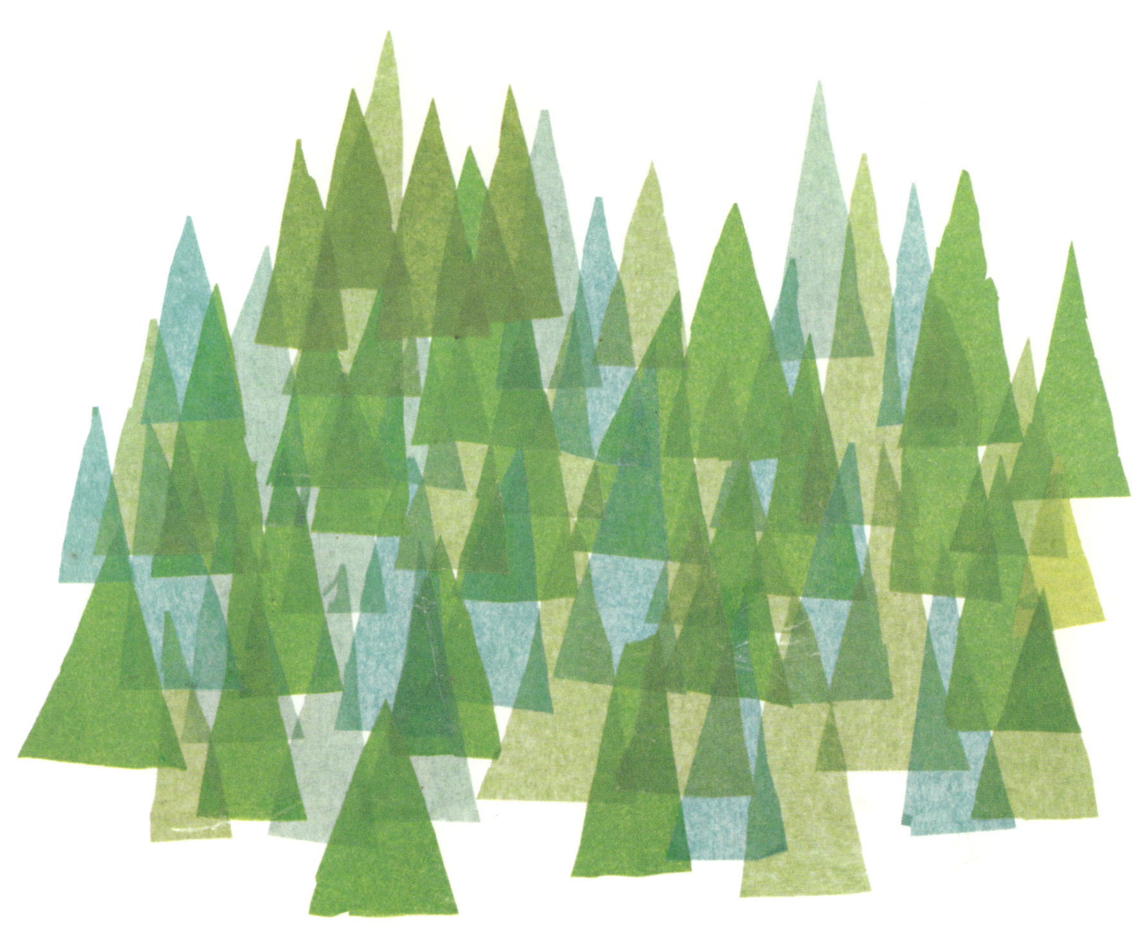

'It looks like a wood.' Composed of triangular transparent elements (boy, 11).
Other elements can be selected to suggest other associations: squares, rectangles, trapezoids, and so forth. For technique, see p. 31.

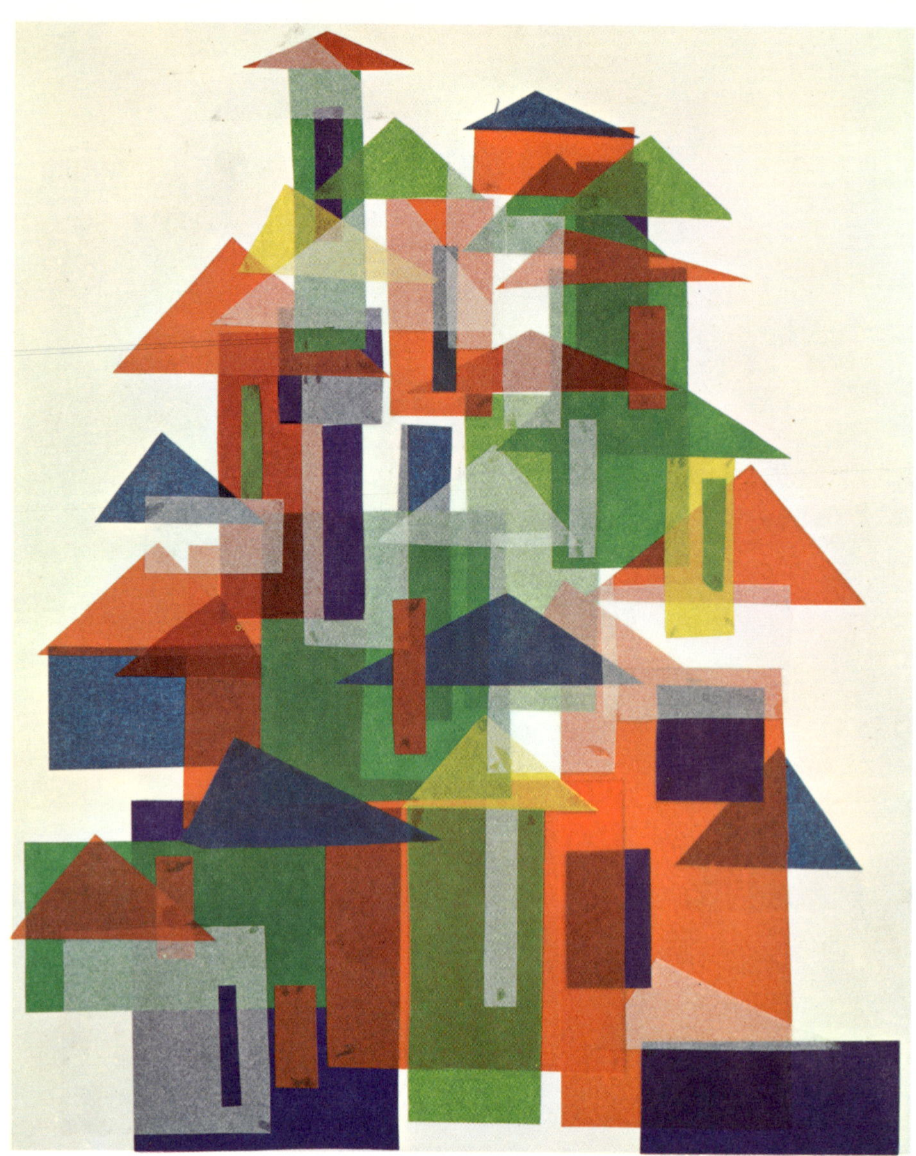

Above:
'Hill of houses.' Coloured tissue paper, cut out and pasted. For technique, see p. 31.

Right:
'Floating shapes in front of verticals and horizontals.' For technique, see p. 31.

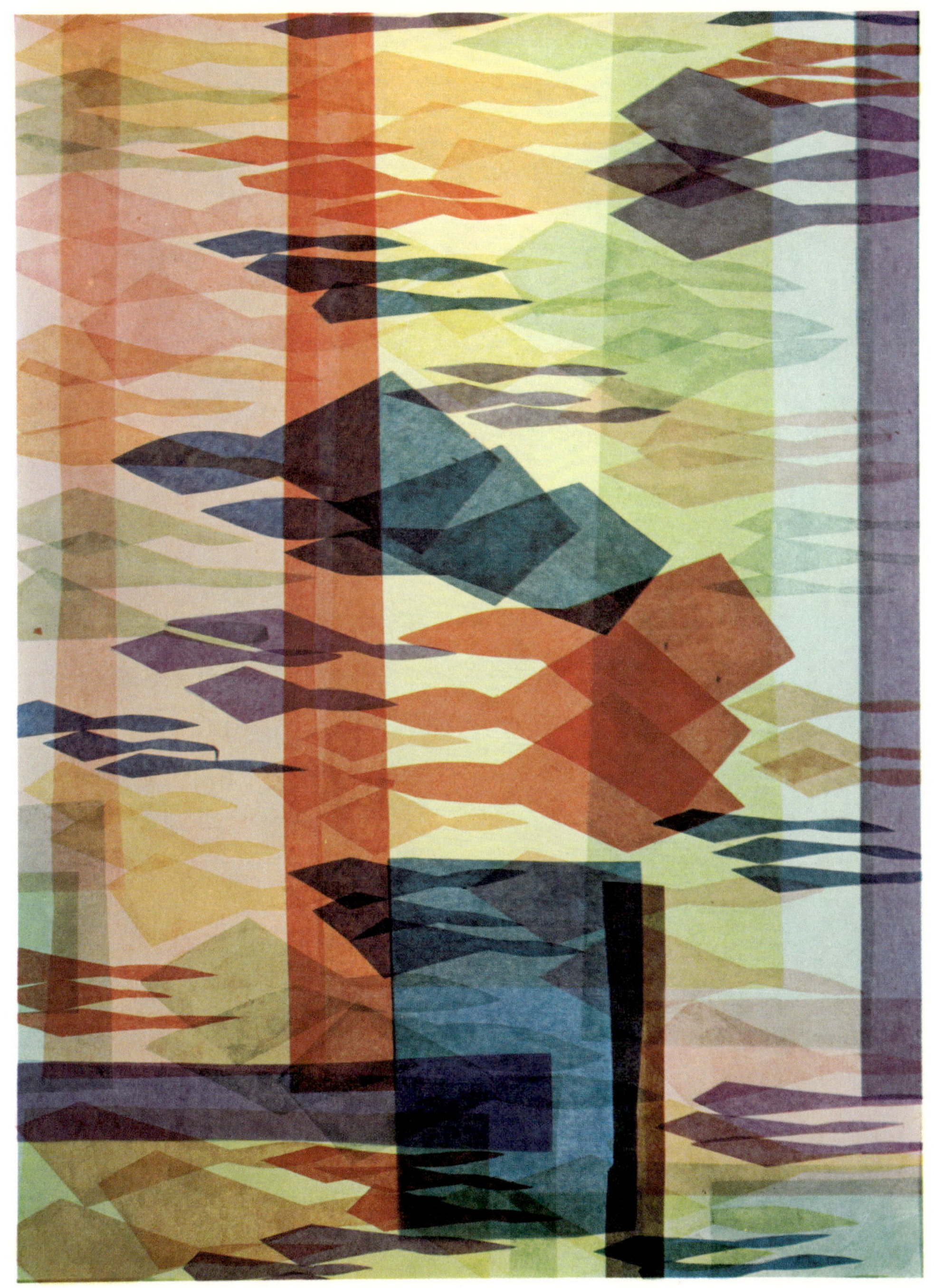

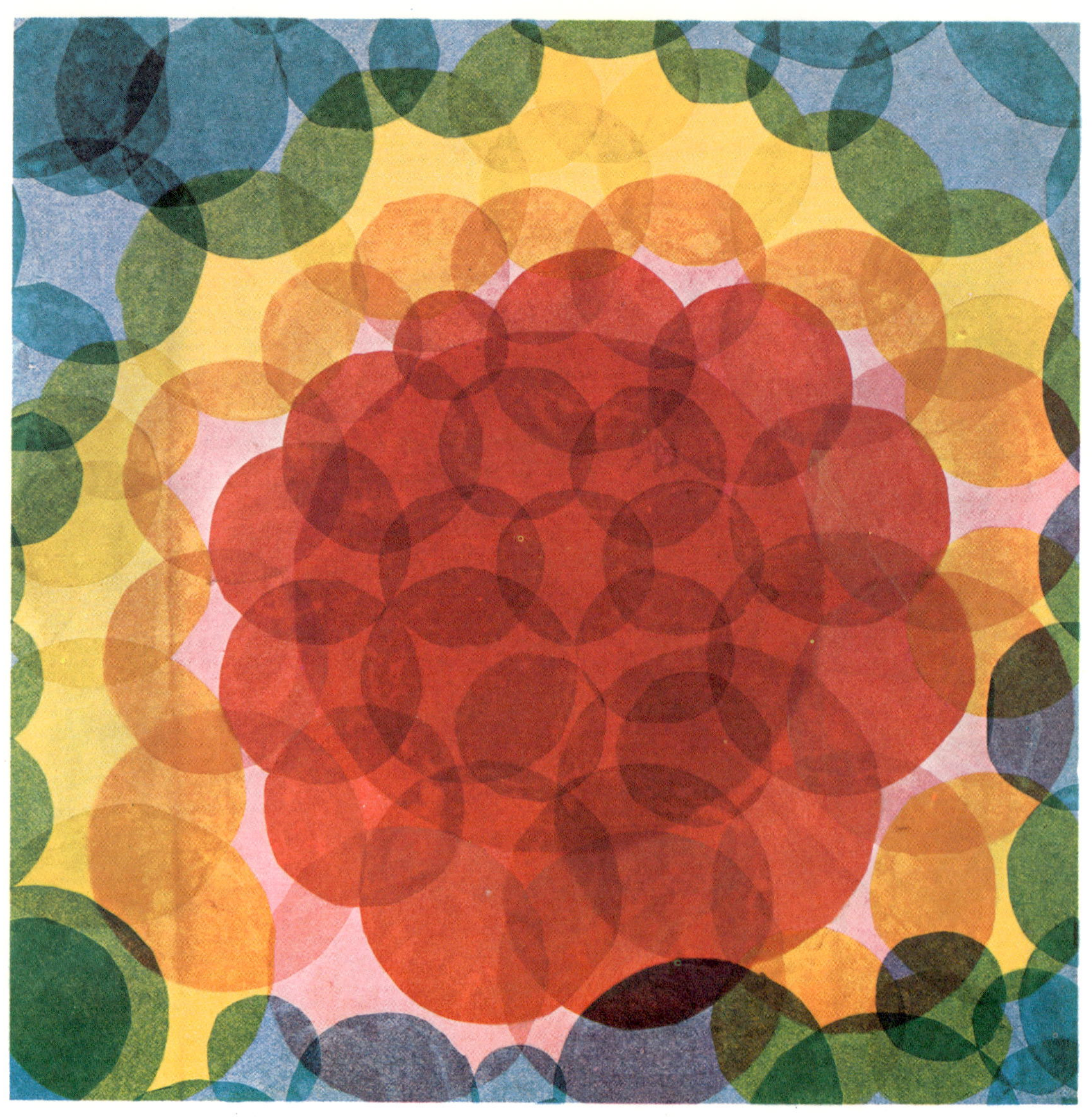

'Rosette.' Transparent collage (girl, 14). Punched out elements go from the red, central point, through yellow and green, to blue. A task for organization and colour differentiation combined. For technique, see p. 36.

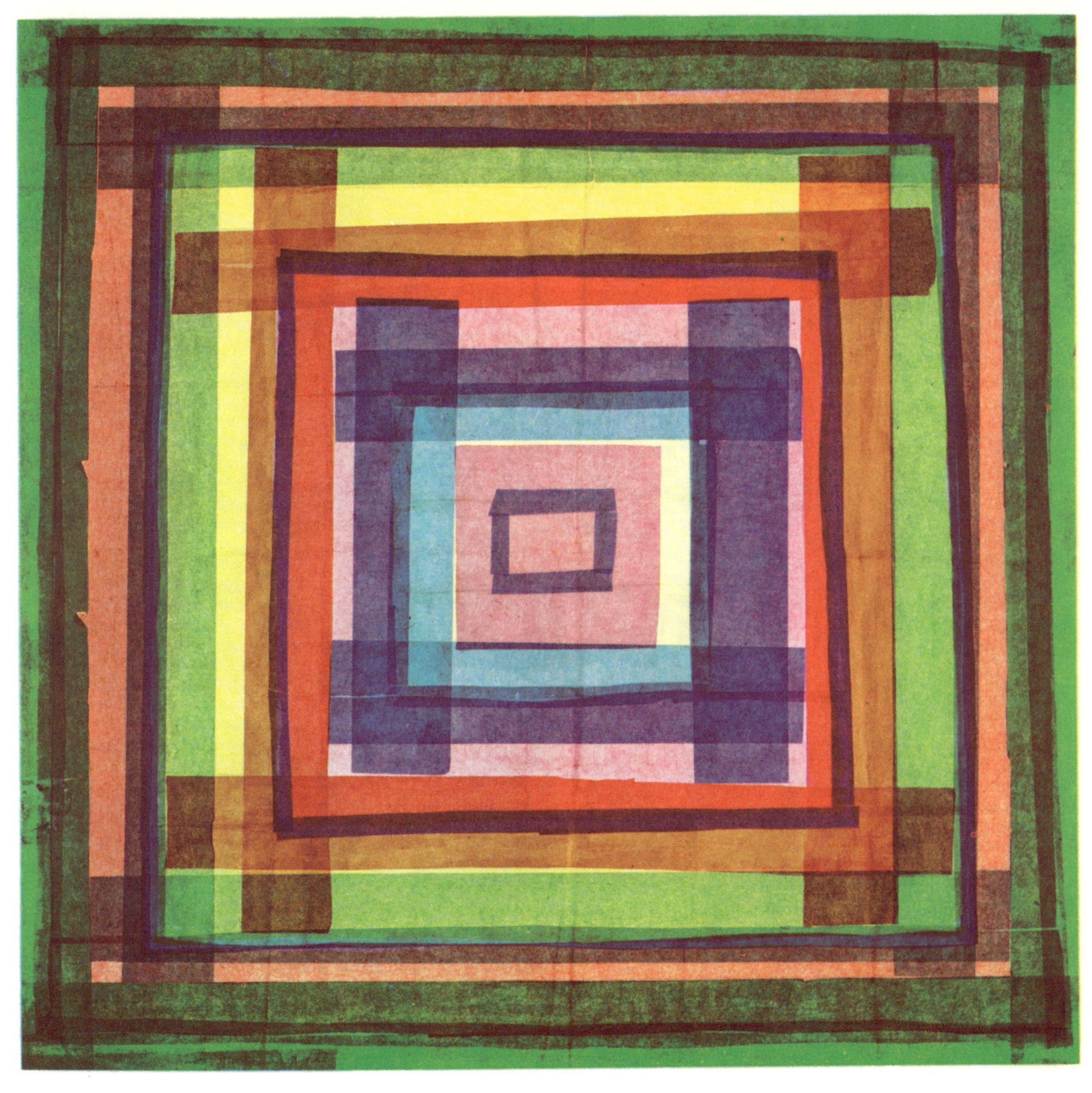

'Central composition.' Transparent paper (girl, 15). For technique, see p. 31.

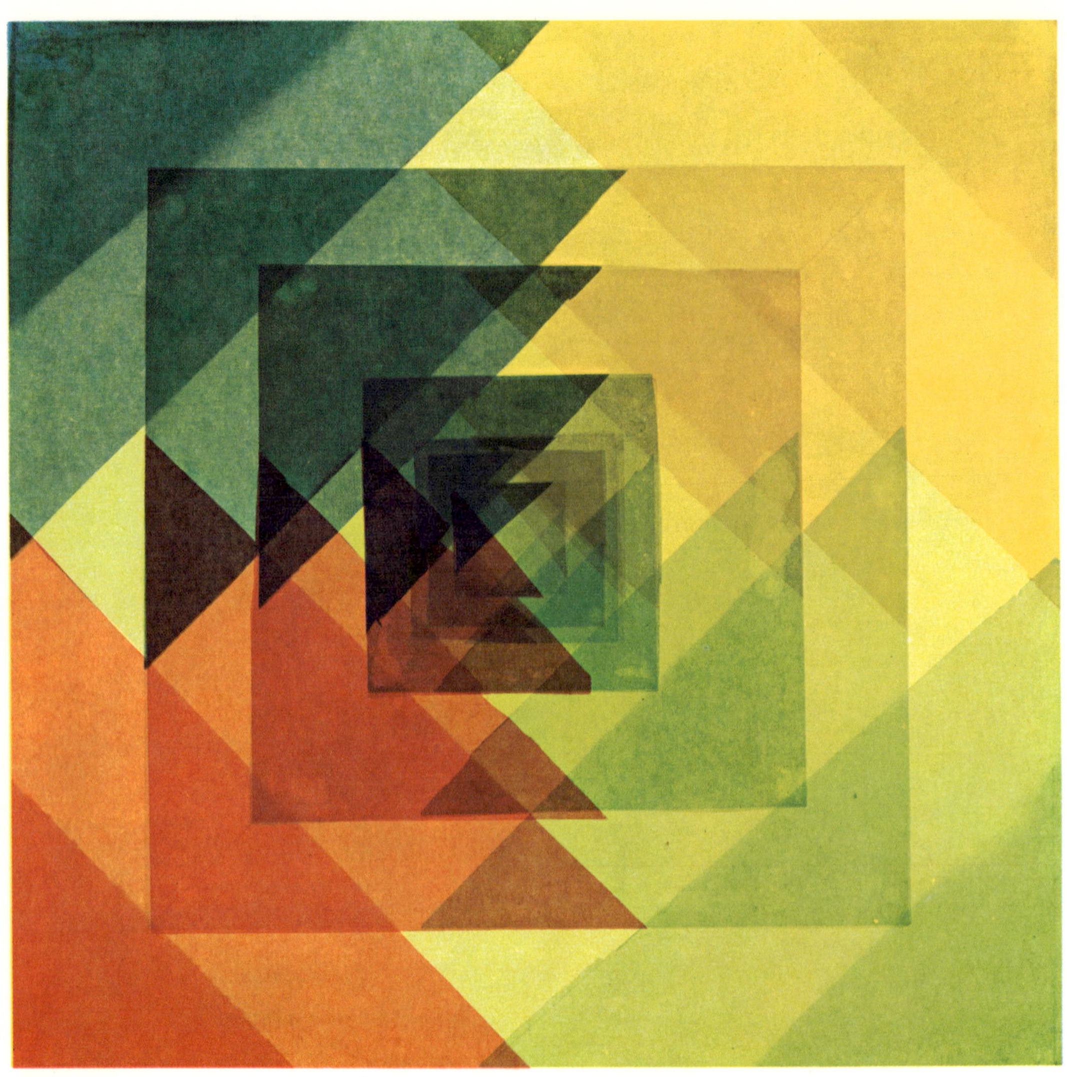

'Colour-cycle composition.' Transparent paper (girl, 15). Obtained with simple means. The pictures on both pages are segments of large window transparencies. Original size 20" square.

Right:
'Ornament' (girl, 16).

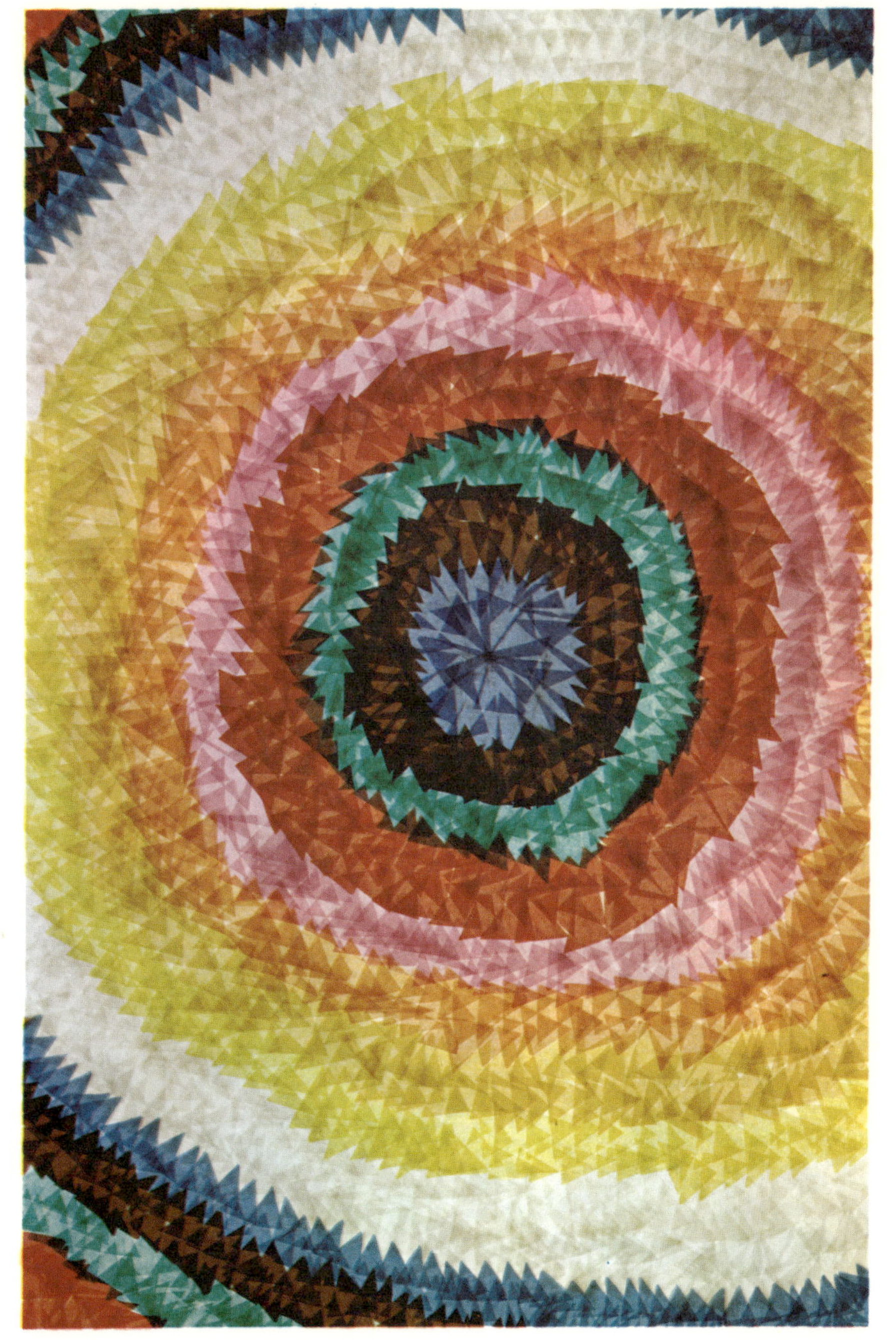

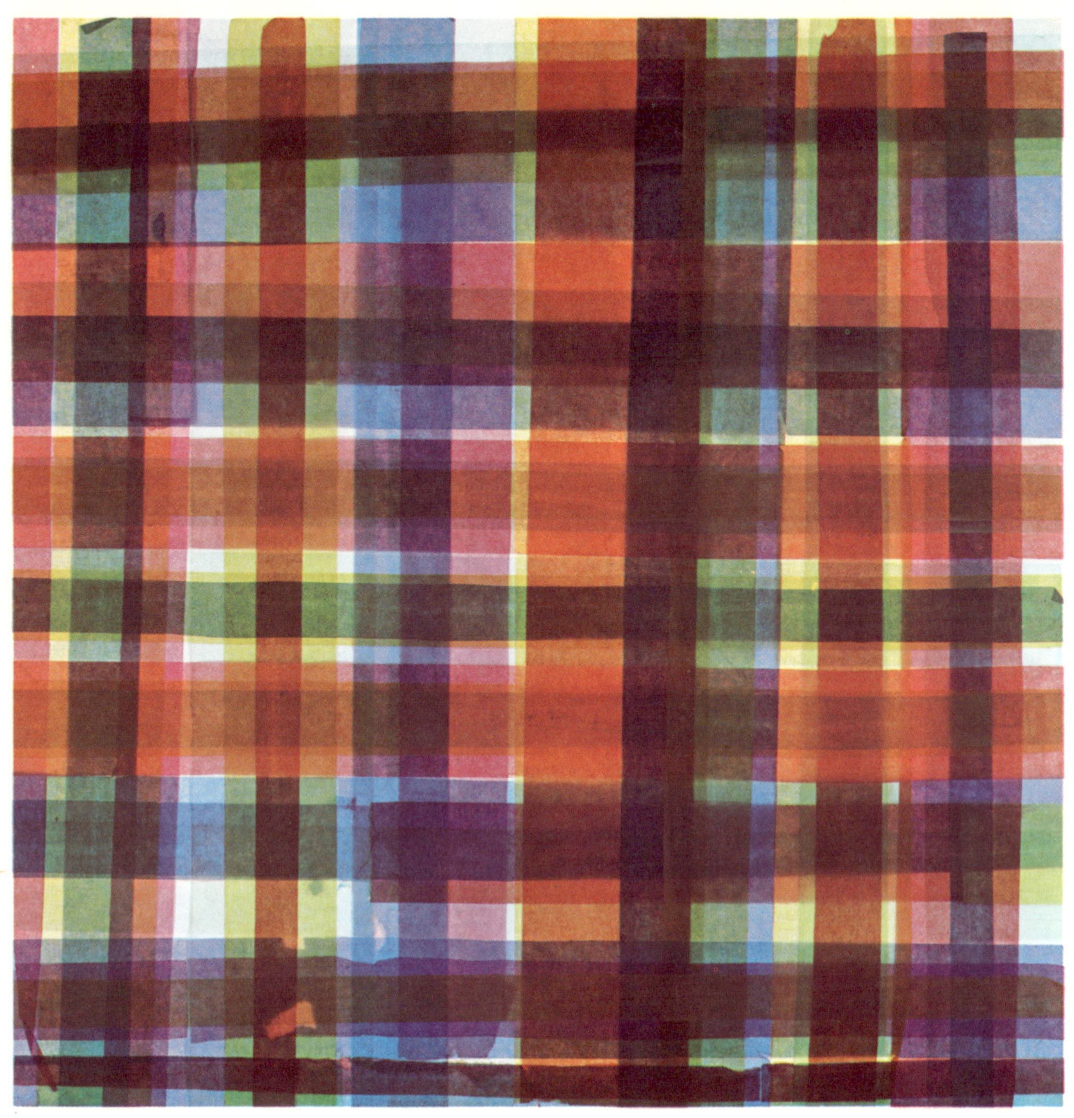

'Stripe composition.' Transparent paper (girl, 13). The colours form an actual mixture in the light. A wealth of subtle shading is revealed. For technique, see pp. 31-33.

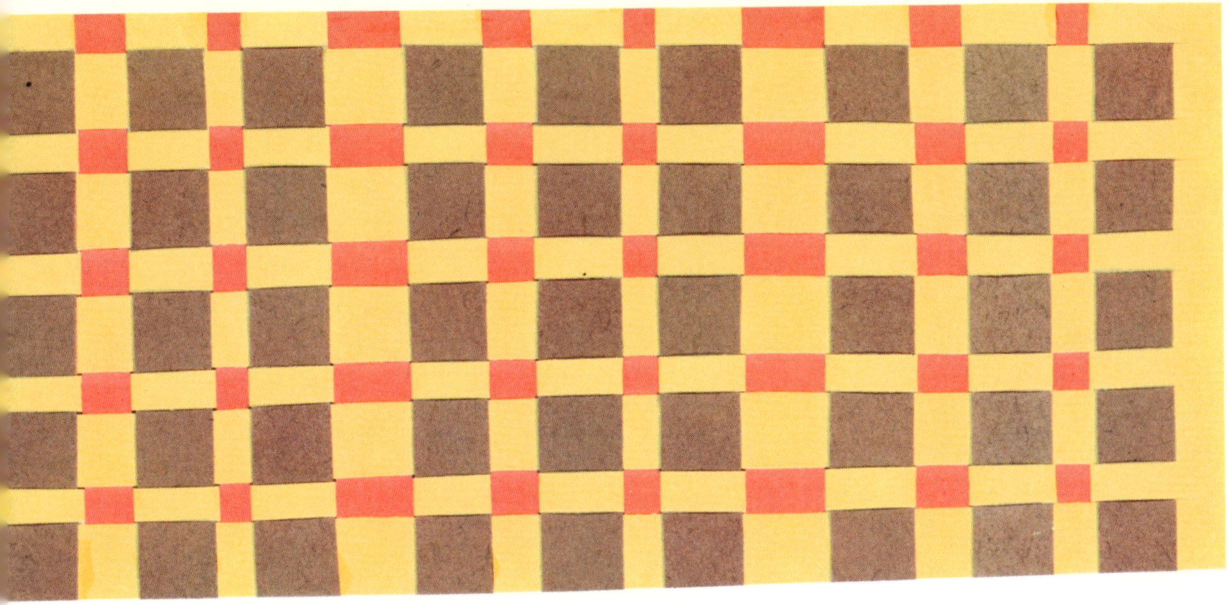

'Weaving with coloured paper' (girl, 10). For technique, see p. 40.

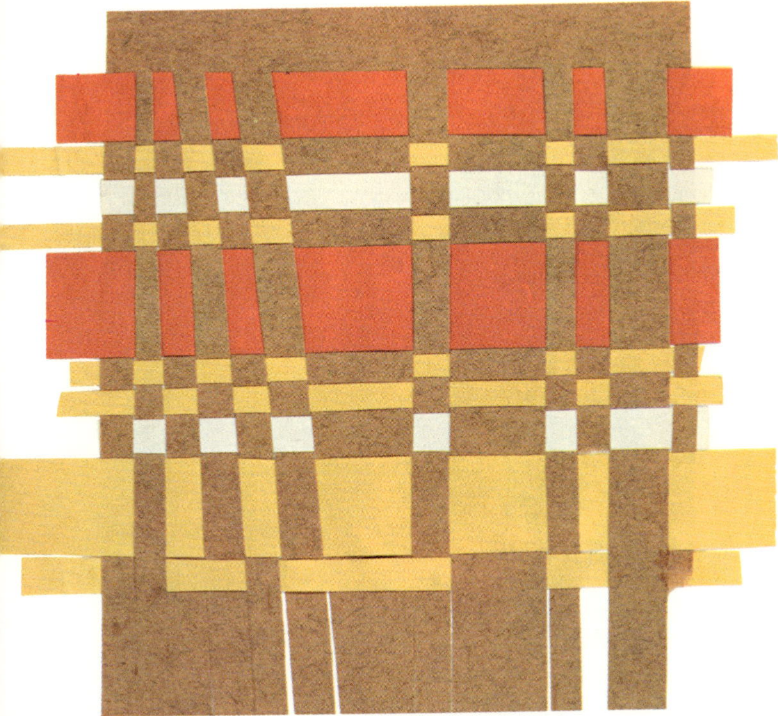

'Weaving with coloured paper' (girl, 14).

Index

Table of Technical Skill Levels for Grades 1 through 9

Not all techniques are suitable for children. Some of them are simply too hard without methodical preparation or require of the child too high a measure of differentiation. The following table is merely intended as a helpful guide in determining which techniques can be offered at each age level. Thus, it depends on the teacher's skill to present the difficult to the small ones without overestimating them, or the easy to the large ones without boring them by underestimation.
The series of numbers refer to the pages.

Grade 1:	7, 9, 12, 20, 40
Grade 2:	7, 9, 12, 20, 40
Grade 3:	7, 9, 10, 11, 12, 14, 20, 29, 30, 31, 40, 42, 46
Grade 4:	7, 8, 9, 10, 11, 12, 14, 18, 20, 29, 30, 31, 32, 33, 40, 41, 42, 46, 48
Grade 5:	7, 8, 10, 11, 12, 14, 15, 17, 18, 19, 20, 22, 23, 24, 26, 27, 29, 30, 31, 32, 33, 35, 40, 41, 42, 43, 45, 46, 48
Grade 6:	7, 8, 10, 11, 12, 14, 15, 17, 18, 19, 20, 22, 23, 24, 25, 26, 27, 28, 30, 31, 32, 33, 34, 35, 36, 37, 38, 39, 41, 42, 43, 45, 47, 48
Grades 7, 8 and 9:	7, 8, 10, 11, 12, 14, 15, 17, 18, 19, 20, 22, 23, 25, 26, 27, 28, 31, 32, 33, 34, 35, 36, 37, 38, 39, 41, 42, 43, 45, 47, 48